The House of Song

The House of Song

POEMS BY
DAVID WAGONER

University of Illinois Press
Urbana and Chicago

Library of Congress Cataloging-in-Publication Data
Wagoner, David.
The house of song : poems / by David Wagoner.
p.   cm.
ISBN 0-252-02730-2 (cloth : alk. paper)
ISBN 0-252-07048-8 (paper : alk. paper)
I. Title.
PS3545.A345H68   2002
811'.54—dc21   2001003999

These poems are all for Adrienne, Alexandra, and Robin
with all my love

Contents

2

3

4

1

The House of Song

He would go to a strange shore
  Where there was no one, and at dawn
   On the fourth day of waiting,
Having eaten little and drunk nothing
  But water, he would draw a square
   In the sand above the tide,
Sit down in it, facing east, and begin. All day
  He would make his song out of the palm leaves,
   Out of the warm wind,
Out of the puzzles of flotsam
  And sea foam. It would startle awake
   And put down roots, would spread
Down into the salt bitterness
  Of the sea, and the first pale-green
   Hard-sheathed stem of a song would rise,
The mouth of its bud still shut. He would fall
  Asleep at times that afternoon and dream
   As vividly as sunlight, and would waken
To the dreamlike light of evening,
  Still fasting, listening. In the brightness
   Of his sleep or in the darkness
Of the waking night, his song would grow
  Out of the sand or down from the empty sky,
   Which were the same now. It would waver
In the wind or move with the surf,
  Which were the same now. He would see it,
   Hear it, and sing it, which were all
The same now, and by morning it would lie there
  Open, and his friends would find him
   There, as he had asked, would come
Carefully near him, would sit and make a fire
  From last year's withered dancing-wreaths
   And the feathers of sea birds,

And while they breathed the smoke, the songmaker
Would sing his song. They would listen
And say, *It is too heavy,*
It is too short, it is too long
And too broken, it is the wrong color,
It is too cold, it is too much
Like last year's song, it has been spoiled by the moon,
It needs more rain, it is cracked
And falling to pieces, it will only be
Beautiful if you hear us, and by sunset
When they had walked away, when their bodies
Had grown smaller and smaller
And disappeared, he would listen to their voices
Again through the night, sleeping
And waking, and in the morning
He would walk back to his village,
Carrying his song in his cupped palms like water
Clear as air, like an open flower
No one could see. The people would wait for him,
Closing their eyes as he stood among them
And sang his song three times.
They would sing it together then,
Even the children, till they had learned it,
Till the costume-makers and dancing-masters
Had learned their shapes and places, how they should all
Rise and gather, open themselves and close
On that day of the yearly feast
A hundred years ago in the Gilbert Islands,
While the songmaker would sit silent
Among them, watching and listening
As the people became that song,
As the whole village around him and around them
Became the house of that song.

Moth Flight

For this moth there is no way
    In the world to fly
        Straight it is so light each wing
Though moving in tandem goes
    Against a different air the slightest
        Difference in an inch
Of breeze will flutter it up
    Or down or off
        Indifferently at an angle
Each time what does it think
    It's doing aiming its antennae so
        Grimly or lightheartedly
In a general direction while being
    Buffeted this way or this
        Other way way off course
And back to where it might have missed
    Its turn a moment ago it's gone
        Again on a centrifugal or centripetal
Tangent the first law of its motion constantly
    Impinged on intercepted
        By winds and half-winds
And their fadeaway offspring
    Who must have no hearts at all
        To break a journey consisting
Almost entirely of detours
    Feints evasive actions it will
        Alight now on a street sign
To rest to think things over to get
    The drift of where it might have been
        Going or been taken or what
It was being taken for perhaps
    To wonder at our two bodies walking
        So unflappably past in straight lines

To our destination having been prearranged
>To intersect each other
>>Here at this intersection
Of more straight lines our purpose lying
>Directly and straightforwardly
>>Before us dated and numbered
Like our evenings together
>Timed by the sunset while this moth now
>>See how fortunately has found
What it hardly knew it was looking for
>Behind us at the foot of a billboard
>>Where it would never have occurred
To us to go in our right minds
>On purpose and has uncoiled the spring
>>Of its tongue to drink at a flowerhead.

The Words-and-Music Men

They said they could make up songs
    Out of anything we could say, right there
      In the lobby before the movie, one old man
At an old upright, the other beside it almost
Dancing. They were daring us, *Come on,*
    So somebody yelled, "Hello!" and the piano
Jangled clinkety-clank plunk-plunk, and those two
    Old words-and-music men sang out together,
      Hello hello again and tapped their shoes
And smiled from under their flat straw hats,
    Tilted toward each other, and sang, *Hello*
    Is all we need and all we know
In green summer suits and bow ties, their false teeth
    Flashing, their crinkled eyes taking us in
      At a glance, *We could have said Good-bye,*
But saying Hello is so much joy you know
    We can only think of today so what we say
      Is Keep on singing tomorrow. My mother and father
Were waiting impatiently. They wanted my body
    To follow them down the aisle right now
      And sit down in the good seats
Before they were all gone. But what I wanted
    Was to stay with the men who could make up music
      About anything, anything. I was trying to think
Of anything, but somebody else said something,
    And the men were singing about pretty girls
      Being hot in June. I wanted to ask them
How they'd learned to stand there and keep grinning
    And daring strangers to think up any words
      They couldn't turn into songs. I wanted to say,
Who are you? How did you ever decide
    To be who you are? I wanted to ask out loud
      And have them sing me an answer,

But louder people were already shouting
The funniest, hardest words they could think of,
And my mother and father were calling
From the doorway to come along this minute
To see the coming attractions, and though I lingered
And heard their jingly finale and saw them
Roll their piano past the popcorn stand,
Sweaty and grim-faced—both looking even older,
Pushing it carefully into a storage room
And shutting it up there, then ducking outside
To breathe in the smoky evening—I've had to imagine
What they might have sung for me: *Who
Are you? And why don't you do what we do?
Just take a word or two and you'll see, you'll see,
Oh boy we're a lot like you.*

For Laurel and Hardy on My Workroom Wall

They're tipping their battered derbies and striding forward
    In step for a change, chipper, self-assured,
        Their cardboard suitcases labeled
Guest of Steerage. They've just arrived at the boot camp
    Of the good old French Foreign Legion
        Which they've chosen as their slice of life
Instead of drowning themselves. Once again
    They're about to become their own mothers and fathers
        And their own unknowable children
Who will rehearse sad laughter and mock tears,
    Will frown with completely unsuccessful
        Concentration, and will practice the amazement
Of suddenly understanding everything
    That baffles them and will go on baffling them
        While they pretend they're only one reel away
From belonging in the world. Their arrival
    Will mark a new beginning of meaningless
        Hostilities with a slaphappy ending. In a moment,
They'll hear music, and as if they'd known all along
    This was what they'd come for, they'll put down
        The mops and buckets given them as charms
With which to cleanse the Sahara and move their feet
    With a calm, sure, delicate disregard
        For all close-order drill and begin dancing.

Wallace Stevens on His Way to Work

He would leave early and walk slowly
    As if balancing books
        On the way to school, already expecting
To be tardy once again and heavy
    With numbers, the unfashionably rounded
        Toes of his shoes invisible beyond
The slope of his corporation. He would pause
    At his favorite fundamentally sound
        Park bench, which had been the birthplace
Of paeans and ruminations on other mornings,
    And would turn his back to it, having gauged the distance
        Between his knees and the edge of the hardwood
Almost invariably unoccupied
    At this enlightened hour by the bums of nighttime
        (For whom the owlish eye of the moon
Had been closed by daylight), and would give himself wholly over
    Backward and trustingly downwards
        And be well seated there. He would remove
From his sinister jacket pocket a postcard
    And touch it and retouch it with the point
        Of the fountain he produced at his fingertips
And fill it with his never-before-uttered
    Runes and obbligatos and pellucidly cryptic
        Duets from private pageants, from broken ends
Of fandangos with the amoeba *chaos chaos*
    Couchant and rampant. Then he would rise
        With an effort as heartfelt as a decision
To get out of bed on Sunday and carefully
    Relocate his center of gravity
        Above and beyond an imaginary axis
Between his feet and carry the good news
    Along the path and the sidewalk, well on his way
        To readjusting the business of the earth.

The Lessons of Water

> The best way to conduct oneself may be observed in the
> behavior of water.
> —Tao Teh Ching

When given a place to wait, it fills that place
By taking the shape of what contains it,
Its upper surface poised and level,
Absorbing, accepting what it can as lightly
Or heavily as it does itself. If pressed
Down, it will offer back in all directions
Everything it was given. If chilled, it will shatter
Daylight and whiten to stars, will harden and sharpen
And turn unforeseeably dazzling. Neglected,
It will disappear, being transformed and lifted
Into thin air. Or thrown away, it will gather
With other water, which is all one water,
And rise and fall, regather and go on rising
And falling the more quickly its path descends
And the more slowly as it wears that path away,
To be left awhile, to stir for the moon, to wait
For the wind to begin again.

Lachrymals

Some Roman women saved their tears in them.
  They held flat narrow-necked heart-shaped delicate phials
    Below their eyelids against each cheek in turn
And caught their tears. No one could shed enough
  In a single spasm to fill that tiny hollow,
    So the women stoppered each with a glass teardrop
And waited. In the meanwhile, some wore them
  Like pendants to have that smooth translucent glass
    (The colors of changing light on the hills)
Nearby all day and all night: none could be certain
  When grief or pain or a sudden abundance
    Of sorrow might come welling into their eyes
Again. When they were full to the brim,
  Some women carried them as charms
    Of remembrance through their lives
And into their tombs, and some would pour them out
  Into quiet streams or onto the bare earth
    And walk away, and some would drink them.

The Four Fates

The Greeks had words for them. They were the Parcae:
The Spinner, the Measurer, and the One with the Scissors,
The three determined, predetermining Sisters,
Who reigned like the Queens of Taste over Man's Fate.

Clotho would gather flax or tow or fleece
And clump it (halfway organized) on the distaff
And pedal the cranky wheel and get that spindle
Spinning, whirling the fuzz-ball into yarn.

Lachesis drew it fine in spite of tangles
And clots and furry lumps, eyeballed a yard,
A foot, or a smidgen by Rule of Thumb-to-Nose
(And on bad days made an inch or an ell of it)

And passed it over to Atropos, who, if it hadn't
Fallen apart already or thinned out
Of its own weight beyond the breaking point
Or frayed itself in two, would give it a snip,

And that was Life. She had, on the one hand,
The bitter end of a knot untied forever;
In the other, the long or short of it; between,
The fatal flaw or the fatal accident.

The fourth Fate was a kind of cleaning lady
Who swept up after them, to whom the gods
And goddesses and heroes and heroines
Paid almost no attention, being absorbed

By their own absorbent loves and propellant lives,
In spinning their own tales, in cutting up
At festivals, in going on and on
About their goings-on, the immortal scandals.

Meanwhile, the cleaning lady sat by her fire
Each night, at loose ends, braiding the loose ends
Into strands and nets, into webs like macrame
And draping them over fields and along roads

And across the roofs of houses into the woods
And over garden walls and under the gardens
And under the wells and over the graveyards
And along the riverbanks and down to the shore

And out to sea with all the shades of the moon
And the rings around the moon and the darkness
Between the rings and the lights of the other threads
Beyond the darkness interwoven with stars.

Forgetting the Magic Words

You thought you had them on the tip
   Of what you thought
      Was your tongue or somewhere
Behind it on a shelf
     Ramshackled between the tiers
      Along the spiral stairs
Of the castle archives—one phrase
   That had at last been cleared
     Of grunts and persiflage
And insubordinate clauses, the charm
   The blind beggar told you
      Was the cure for everyone
And every wrong, for those left standing
   And waiting at the crux
     Of the plot (the princess
In chains, the villain, the monster)
   For you to usher them
      With a smile to a happy ending,
But impatient now, they see you
   Here, your mouth slumped open
     For suggestions from the floor
Or the ceiling or the corners
   Of the dungeon, and soon they'll go on
     To their grisly end without you.

High Steel

The path ahead of you is the upper serif
　　Of an I-beam, a rigid girder
　　　　Riveted, secure, as stable
As the earth and the next wind
　　Will allow. But you don't quite
　　　　Believe it, do you. You think you're here
To examine the view or the lofty poise
　　Of the overhead crane, to visualize
　　　　Fire escapes and curtain walls
Or to calculate how far you may be off
　　The ground. Instead, you've decided you simply must
　　　　Walk on a surface no more likely
To wobble under you
　　Than a sidewalk. You're not inclined
　　　　To stagger, are you? You're wearing shoes.
You're trailing no loose ends.
　　So all that's required of you is (easy now)
　　　　To put one shaky foot ahead
Of the other and to follow
　　That terribly simple-seeming good example
　　　　With the rest of you. You needn't depend
On anyone but yourself to cooperate
　　In an act you've been performing for the bulk
　　　　Of your life: conducting your leg bones
Under your torso without changing your mind
　　Or your definition of progress.
　　　　So why are you half-crouching
There, flushed at the knees, your arches
　　As depressed as your soles, holding
　　　　Your semiprecious center of gravity
Too heavily or too lightly from one moment
　　To the next? As a higher mammal
　　　　Descended from those who first presumed

To take an upright posture and aimed themselves
Forward and took a step in the right direction
With only a second thought,
Why are you leaning backward and hanging on
And shutting your eyes against what's obviously
Waiting dead ahead?

Aerial Act

Suspended from darkness (beyond her
　　Only the needle-thin glitter
　　　　Of guy-wires) she swings so far
Upward, she's nearly flying back
　　To her beginning, the whole circumference
　　　　Of her centrifugal dance
Forward to pause in the bright cone of the light
　　That tries to follow her backward into suspense
　　　　And in and out of the glare
Of her flashing spangles. The catcher
　　As predictable as a pendulum
　　　　Is ready to meet her upside down at the end
Of what the announcer booms will be
　　A never-before-attempted three and a half
　　　　Somersaults under this very roof. Her hair
In a swirling braid and her bare feet
　　Pointed, she holds firm to the level bar
　　　　And almost at its highest, oh, she lets go
And revolves against her knees and her tucked ankles
　　And spins in a trajectory arching down,
　　　　Springs at full length and reaches her empty arms
Toward the arms that should appear
　　Against the rapidly turning heaven and earth
　　　　And the loud horizon, each with its own
Bedazzled vital message. She has become
　　Only her eyes, straining to touch, only
　　　　Her fingers opening
To grasp the extended arms
　　Of the other welcoming
　　　　Her to the beginning
Of their joint venture. But their hands
　　Glance by each
　　　　Other by inches,

And she keeps on falling
    In a steepening curve. We have
    A split moment
Now to wonder why
    She's going to die so gracefully
    For some purpose we have no time
To understand, so brief and strange
    A fulfillment. But joining palms
    Like a diver, bowing her head, her chin
Touching her breastbone, her light
    Wingless birdlike body extends
    And levels perfectly to meet
The narrow net which suddenly settles her
    More slowly down almost against the ground,
    Then bears her up and tosses her to her feet
And yields to her as she lopes to the hard edge,
    Kneels, swivels, and lets herself stand again
    On sawdust and walk away into the shadows.

On Thin Ice

This is the smoothest going, you've put yourself
Forward, slithering, not from toe to heel
Like an ordinary walker through a snowfall
Light as the evening light but gracefully
Like a dancing master giving a demonstration
Of gliding to beginners, you exercise
Restraint and your body simultaneously
With only an occasional slipshod
Sidestep choreographed by chance, and you present
Your compliments to the character you've become
For whom no path is forbidden, for whom walking
On air or water is not confined to dreams
But part of a footloose climate of agreement.

You hear a groan. The ice has given a groan
At your weight, as you have yourself. You give
Slightly at the knees, sometimes a sign in the past
Of giddiness, faint-heartedness, the fault-finding
Of earth, or the grudging, half-appalled intention
Of humbling yourself before a greater power
Like fatigue or gravity.
                    Then it all gives in
Under your feet suddenly, oh, you have
That sinking feeling, your ankles, your shinbones,
Your knees, your thighs, your hips, your diaphragm,
Your ribs, your clavicles, your neck, your chin,
Your mouth, your nose, your eyes, your forehead, the last
Diminishing circle of scalp, and even the ends
Of your thinning hair usurped by water colder
Than any remembrance, you have broken through
Into a lost dimension which receives you
With an almost frozen reluctance and then slowly

Shows you the way into the light
Where you spread your arms and brace yourself in a hole
Of your own devising.
                    Simply clambering out
By thrashing and main force, by giving thin ice
Hell, what for, by slapping and scrabbling at it,
Will get you nowhere faster than you think,
So you turn your back and lift your face to the sky
And float your body level again and stroke
For shore against the gradually more firm
Edge of the break till it can bear your shoulders
And eventually all of you and maybe
Even before you're on solid ground again
It may put up with you on your own two legs,
Slopping, skidding, and toddling waterlogged
And heavily laden now onto dry land,
Stiffening toward home, your feet on the ground.

Landscaping Rocks for Sale

They look like what they are: wreckage, the offspring
Of explosions in the mountains, some still caught
In the act of colliding, slamming into each other,
Split images of themselves in this vacant lot,
All broken and in need
Of more breaking, outcasts, parts of a puzzle
Never to be resolved.

They seem like the embodiment of faction,
Dissatisfaction, cleavages, like upholders
Of permanent grudges, crackpots, splinter groups,
Perpetuators of raw dichotomies,
Schizoid blockheaded squatters
Whose purpose in life or death is putting it bluntly
To occupy space
And have done with everything and everybody,
Even their likenesses, and to hell with it,
Though some stand alone, jagged, in place, out of place,
Out of it, in an emergency ward
Of rocks, done for.

But in one corner, a dozen river stones
The shades of the under-sky through a spring of storms
Lie at their ease as if the current were still
Running over and over them, still taking
Their time away from them one grain at a time
And leaving as slowly
And swiftly there a time more durable
Than ever, to be lifted
Out of the light of earth into our darkness
And a hard beginning.

The Landscaper

He comes with the deal, he tells me, his services
    Come with the new house, and he's taking orders,
        So what do I want? Now, how about azaleas
And some rhodies here and here. A couple of sweetgums?
    But I have to understand he's on a budget
        With a sonofabitch
Of a contractor who don't want to pay nothing
    To nobody. How would I like a windbreak
        Of blue-green cypress stuck from here to there
To shut off my neighbor? I suggest maybe
    It wouldn't be right to shut anybody off,
        But he says fuck 'em, make an embankment,
Against the runoff of rain here on this slope
    And soak my own lawn good. Now how much grass
        Do I want? I consider the plot—
Less than a tennis court—and try to imagine
    Grass, but he's doing a summer sales dance
        From stake to stake. I can have perennials
Here and here and right along here,
    And he stamps the ground, becoming bowlegged bushes
        And shrubs and clumps and going hopping mad
Like Rumpelstiltskin stomping and growing roots
    From the lively soles of his feet, like the man with the power
        To spring my bulldozed dirt to life again
And put the rest in the shade. He can stick a pine
    Smack up against a rock, but he won't plant it
        Straight like an idiot. He starts them
Crooked so when they grow they look like me
    And him, you know, like they haven't had it easy.
        And he looks at me and says he hopes I know
I get a front yard only. What's in the back
    Is strictly up to me. And we both stand there
        On what was once the business end of a glacier

That tumbled the rubble of empty neighborhoods
        Around and around and smoothed them into beds
        And buried them in unpopulated streams
When it melted away north
        And let the people through. He can put rocks
            In here, he says, big rocks, little rocks,
Natural-looking rocks. Do I like rocks? I tell him
        Yes, I like river stones. They seem at home
            No matter where they are or where they've been,
No matter what grows beside them. And right there,
        Before his very eyes, I almost turn
            Into one for him, and we shake on it.

The Joggers

The three women in jogging suits come thumping
   Along the asphalt out of step
      And sorts and breath, all nursing
Grudges against the earth, which keeps calling them
   Down too hard against it, making their knees
      Give and give without giving, making
What occupies them under the Spandex
   And floppily loose sweatshirts
      Rise and fall too far. They seem determined
To go straight on through this development
   In spite of the steady eyes of the carpenters
      And framers keeping track of them, who don't say
Anything out loud. The women are not quite
   Ready to give up. They're exchanging fragments
      From their domestic scenes—the extra-
Curricular requirements of class size
   And the bare community chest. Their shoes
      Are not living up to half the promises
Of their names and logos. Now they're cutting across
   A corner lot with new-laid strips of lawn
      Like slices of green cake, and suddenly
The sprinklers go on. Arches of sputtering water
   Go sailing and carousing around them
      In laggardly swirls to sprinkle up and over
Their hair and shoulders, a geometric rain
   Like magical chandeliers whose candle flames
      Are flying prisms of sunlight. They shriek
And clutch their own arms first, but then reach out
   For each other and try to scamper
      Sideways and backward and go bumping
Ahead, lifting their knees like storybook girls
   Alarmed by mice. But just as abruptly
      They let their shoulders and arms fall down and out

With a graceful nonchalance, and all three,
　　With one consent, begin laughing and singing,
　　　　Their arms lifting like wings. Their glistening shoes
Go tripping lightly and easily, rising
　　And falling together, as they join hands
　　　　Like the familiar spirits of a fountain.

A Girl Playing in a Sandbox

She drops the plastic soldiers, the trucks
And tanks and caissons over the side
Of the sandbox and begins smoothing
The field of battle with her hands and forearms,
Sweeping away the foxholes, trenches, and craters
Where only a moment ago the lost patrols
And panzers had plowed to the four known corners
Of her desert under the leadership
Of boys. She follows her own fingers
With her eyes as if she could see the wind
Retouching the dunes, as if she could hear it
Trembling along the sand, the lovely fragments,
The cracked misshapen incongruously melded
And bedded abrasive multitudes, the ruins
Of mountains, now bringing themselves
More peacefully together around her, obeying
Her slightest gesture and changing everything
They are, for her alone, at her lightest touch.

God and Man and Flower

Flower in the crannied wall,
I pluck thee out of the crannies.
I hold you, root and all, in my hand,
Little flower,—but if I could understand
What you are, root and all and all in all,
I would know what God and man is.
    —Alfred, Lord Tennyson

But, my dear lord, now that it's in your hand,
What are you going to do with it? The roots
Of a windblown seed had groped sideways
Into flagstone crannies, grappling for root-holds
And root-room in a bent world. Its stem had come curving
Outward and upward from that bleak hardscrabble
Somehow poised, keeping its balance, to open
A small mouth to the light.

And now you've wrenched it loose, the sandgrains
And darker matter crumbling away from it,
And you hold it up to your nose, musing,
Then drop it into the gravel at your feet
Where it can wither and wilt at its leisure
While you continue your stroll, not understanding
What the flower knows: it is a fearful thing
To fall out of the hands of the living god.

Dr. Frankenstein's Garden

He needed a place where he could clean his hands
    By getting them dirty; by handling the raw clay
      Before it caught its breath
And broke its mold, a place for a humbler kind
    Of recreation, somewhere less public
      Than a graveyard. He wanted to look
More closely at more understandable roots,
    Not the short-lived messy short-circuited
      And finally unknowable loose ends
Of nervous systems dwindling
    To less than nothing in dead meat
      And bones better left to dogs
Than to a laboratory. He sent his servants
    To all the nurseries to fetch whatever seedlings
      Had grown indifferent to sunlight
(His walls were high) and independent of drains
    (His were all spoken for), whatever was given
      To occult behavior or cryptic flowering,
Specimens likely, maybe, to kill their neighbors
    But only out of exuberance, only by exceeding
      Even their hardiest, wildest expectations,
By crowding or by overshadowing others,
    By getting above themselves or beside themselves.
      He dreamed of being alone there, standing
By a pool of water, astonished, fondling
    The green surprises when they rose around him
      And opened their sweet mouths
As if at any moment he might be
    Transformed into a moth or a butterfly,
      A source and a receiver. It had to be
A sanctuary he could remember with pleasure
    While cat-and-mouse-napping at his desk
      Or bending over a monster, somewhere

To get away from it all, a kind of silence
        In the back of his noisy mind. Didn't all gods
                Long for and nurture that, if they had a mind to?
But after a rainy night, his novices
        Sprang up full grown, spreading and stumbling
                Over moniliform feet with scabrous spikelets
And hispid tendrils, suckers and cling-tights.
        They made him earn each meditative step
                By biting and snagging, by groping with hold-fasts
Up and around his shins like spiral stairs
        And clumping inside his smock. Some thickets
                Had already gone to seed and were scattering
Gossamer-tufted versions of themselves
        To be fluffed and broadcast in the breeze,
                Miasma to miasma. Some were lurching
And shambling down the steps into his dungeon,
        And some were climbing the wall and running away
                Downslope among bare boulders, not bothering
To unhinge the gate and only pausing
        Long enough now and then to branch out sideways
                And break into blossom as if into manic laughter.

The Collectors

At the edge of the woods in the warm night, the collectors
    With a white sheet stretched between them and a lantern
        Hanging behind it have been waiting
For the moths to come, and now they're fluttering
    Out of the darkness to hover
        And catch at the glowing whiteness: the pandoras
And handmaids, the penitent underwings
    And the wood nymphs, the dianas and silks,
        The hairstreaks, daggers, and loopers,
The eye-spotted sphinxes gathering
    And touching in quivering blurs, their silhouettes
        Suspended here and clinging to a light
They couldn't have dreamed of
    On the undersides of leaves in the green sun
        Or through the slants and sleights of the full moon,
And now the collectors' forceps lift away
    The delicate specimens
        And place them carefully (to do no harm
To the scales) in the appropriate killing jars—
    The plaster of paris soaked in cyanide
        Or the cotton and ether—or necessarily
Sometimes a pinching
    Of thoraxes between finger and thumb
        For an instant end, though a few
Must be held there gently
    But firmly for long moments
        Before their wings hold still, before they become
As pliant and recognizable
    As they're required to be, impaled
        Under glass, one-sided and orderly. How else
Could we be certain how
    Remarkable they are? Now we can see them
        Motionless. Now we can all agree

On their names and numbers, on their strangely
And perfectly prearranged markings,
And now we can almost all understand
Their natures and their places in nature
Instead of simply letting them go and go on
Fumbling there uncertainly in the shadows.

Benjamin Franklin and the Dust Devil

As he leaned from the coach window, jouncing and gaping
    And trying to keep his eyes on the Wild Event
        Whirling itself a hundred yards away,
He told the driver to stop. And lurching forward
    Along with the ladies and other gentlemen
        (Who would have preferred not being interrupted
Half in a Pennsylvania ditch), he hazarded
    The first step out and down, his buckled legs
        Adventuring on behalf of Natural Science
And already running after the djinn-sized inverted
    Truncated cone of dust and debris suspended
        By some invisible puppet-master, zigzagging
Like him across the field. With a measured trot
    Intended to keep his hat and hair in place
        He followed its leaps and shifts as it teetered loosely
This way and that, off-balance, a whirlpool
    Of air as turbulent as the affairs of men
        And women and state. Though his notebook remained
Shut in his coat pocket, he made note
    Of the contents of this evanescent giant
        But suddenly saw they were no longer there
(As it puffed itself up and disappeared)
    But here at his feet, all scattered
        Like the loot of a trash collector. Having been himself
A curiosity examined and reexamined
    And speculated upon by all who met him,
        He understood the nature of his desire
To unwind the coil of this eccentric wind
    Before it vanished. Yet he climbed to his seat
        Where the passengers, sullen and scolding now,
Were urging him to recover from his fit,
    To resume his nap and his dignity and the direction
        Of Forward Progress, feeling none the wiser.

The First Passenger Balloon Ascension, 1783

The Brothers Montgolfier were longing
    To float away into the sky
        In their balloon. They'd watched that bubble
Go up all by itself and sail till its air
    Cooled off and the baggy canvas
        Crinkled and shrank, then settled
Down again to dump its basket
    Gently on the ground. But they were afraid
        They couldn't breathe up there
In that windy emptiness
    Among the clouds. Though they weren't sure
        What they wanted to do aloft
Except look down on France
    From a new direction, they needed to be certain
        They could reach the heights
And keep on being themselves. So they gave the honor
    Of first flight to a duck
        Latched in a cage, a rooster,
And a sheep and sent them up with a shove,
    A wave, and a shout, and that globe
        In its net of ropes, as if still breathing
Fire, took off and lifted its passengers
    Over the heads of the crowd. They saw it
        Drift away as high as the pinnacle
Of their hopes through the thinning atmosphere,
    And far in the sky the rooster announced the beginning
        Of endless dawn spurred on by the bright gold
Standard of the sun. He crowed and flapped
    From the dizzy edge of the basket
        While down on the floorboards the sheep
From a sheep's-eye view saw the new world
    Chiefly as willow laths and sisal
        And a firmament made slippery under hoof

By the calls of his nature, and when the rooster
        Trod on his neck, he asserted
            The ancient rights of pasturage
And broke the rooster's elbow. The duck behind bars,
        Who understood which way the balloon and the wind
            Were blowing at every moment but had no room
To spread himself or his wings, withdrew in protest,
        And when the hot air cooled
            And the baggy sack collapsed
Into itself, dwindled and dandled
        Down, across, and into a wheatfield
            And all the important and unimportant people
Came running to celebrate
        The safe return of their heroes and regathered
            That night to quack and cackle and bleat
And stand together in honor of the ascent
        And the heavenly first light breaths
            Their three compatriots had quaffed
Above the clouds, the Brothers Montgolfier
        Beheaded them and cooked them
            And served them to a host of friends, took courage
From their hearts and swore to follow
        Just as gallantly up through the suddenly
            More free, more common, and more fraternal air.

Meeting the Ditchdigger

For an hour, our small black galvanized terrier
Has been whining nose to nose with a glass door,
Not quite barking, chewing the wild cud
Of her longing to give her all to the spectacle
Of a man digging a ditch in our backyard.

Her glances urge me to believe there's someone
There, on her property, digging a hole so deep
And so long across her grass and gravel (the marked
And daily remarkable ground of her whole being),
He has to be categorically disemboweled.

She can't quite swallow the fact that I'm not going
To throw myself out the door immediately
With all the momentum of portable arms and legs
And a voice nearly as rawboned and high-wired
As hers to put a stop to this outrage.

I tell her by preliterate noise and gesture
That all's well, that laying drainpipe is not
Inherently offensive and certainly next to nothing
To be exercised about if you can help it,
That it isn't wise for us to confer right now

In our current states of mind with this other digger
(Being well paid to show the week-long rain
The way to the nearest exit), that he doesn't
Need our aid or comfort or our six feet
Dancing or taking attendance on his mud.

But at last, because her soul-filled psychotope
Is a Fenced Backyard with Intruders of Any Species
(Including Imaginary), because she's bitten
Nothing but toys and food and her own tail,
And because I'm feeling a fraction of her impulse,

I let us both outside. She runs full speed
To the scene of the crime, but then skids to a halt
Five feet short, bristles, crouches, blossoms,
And utters her combination war cry, mother lode
Placer discovery-claim, and life-or-death rattle.

The upper half of the digger stands erect,
And smiling at us like a delegate
From the worldwide Congress of Laborers Out of Love,
He slaps the palm of his work-glove flat on the brink
Of crisis, and she crawls forward to surrender.

Slug

I moved his stone. I turned his house
    Upside down in the garden. Now he's gliding
        Away, his one and only foot
Absorbed by the dry dull aggregate concrete
    Of our patio, having chosen out of all
        Directions the worst for an inchling
Who must make his own way from scratch
    By rippling, glistening, and corrugating
        Along a path no one could love
But him: his own mucus. That shining begins
    Where he was and ends where he is
        At this moment and will end again
Wherever he gives up. The whole nine yards
    Ahead of him would seem to cost more
        Than he can utter. Somewhere roughly
At the point of no return, he will run out
    Of wherewithal and wither
        To a harder, more abrupt version
Of himself, even more distasteful
    To predators than his nature called for,
        And I kneel here, his guilty gardener,
With a multitude of other stones
    He might have had without asking,
        Each one as dank, as ripe for visions
As his other underworld. He goes zigzagging,
    Carrying with him steadily and whole
        Under the horned end of his mantle
The burden of a single opening
    For mouth and anus and for the frank exchange
        Of views between His and Hers. No doubt,

He has brooded androgynously on comings
And goings beneath some balled-up Spenglerian
Nugget of time-death, but what else
Has he been taught in that darkness? Fear
Like Roethke's? Desperation? The daily
Crumbs of bravado? Humiliation?
The principles of uncertainty? How to sleep
At all under the heaviness of his own
Impending despair? After an hour
In what should have been lethal sunlight,
He doesn't seem to think so. He has arrived
At the far edge of a journey I had thought
Beyond him, to the dropping-off place—five inches
Down to lumps of earth where firmament dwindles
To a slough of rain-soaked fill-dirt
And river stones, where even before sundown
He may find another abyss with enough room
For all souls and slugs to nurse their wisdom.

Meditation

Perhaps I could write meditations under a rock in a shower.
—Thoreau, *Journal*, 1857

You won't squirm a path
Easily through that crawl space
Or find yourself at home
On arrival underneath
A sodden heavyweight
Heaven, but just suppose
You've wormed your way
There and found breathing room
By a wood louse or some closer
Kindred broodling. Don't you
Still seem sure to mull
And be mulled (in darkness
And the surrounding rain)
Illegibly in a mind's eye
Illuminated thus far only
Glumly, without a sign
Of the calyx of God's flower
Or whirlwind, let alone
Thunderous transmigration
Into a cooler phylum?

It may be far less trouble
Simply to be good
And do good and feel
Better than to think
Of anything wonderful
To recall in the aftermath
Of your shower when you crawl out
From under and take your place
Again in the bald daylight,
Having earned yourself no horns

Or multiple coats of arms
And legs in the brotherhood
Of mud and having learned
So little, not even os-
Mosis, but merely having
Grown just that much further
Accustomed to being more
Or less of your own kind.

The Weather Man

To learn his fate for the day, he only needed
    To look at the sky and hold out his hand
      And brace himself and wait
For his near future. It was strewn overhead
    In systems billowing their chaotic ways
      Under and over each other, masses and whorls
And sudden serene monstrous emptiness
    Hour after day after night after weeks
      And seasoning into years. Though he might stand
In the dead eye of calm, its only pupil,
    Far out of sight around him the wind was toppling
      Whatever else stood still, was blowing it
Inside out and whistling it to pieces,
    Was spiraling in and grinding away hometowns,
      Upending and flattening anything
And everything, and even in the balmy breathless
    Flutter of a tropical breeze at evening
      When the sun was melting slowly across the sea
Beyond a reef, beyond what seemed to him
    The last place on earth, he might suddenly break
      Into flashes of lightning
From cloud to treetop or out of the top of his skull
    Into black cumulus made manifest
      Around his shoulders and crackle and find himself
Reassembled, covered with dew in a garden
    At the mercy of an atmosphere
      That had no mercy, till he had no heart
At all for any weather and would lie down
    Under a roof and feel the storm still growing
      In moving circles tightening around him,

Brightening and then darkening with fog
And wood smoke, with waves of sea mist,
With the promise of ice and stars
Across his window, drifting together now
Into an interstellar sameness or a forecast
Of morning and ceiling zero.

A Homily for the Preservation of the Spirit in a Time of Dread

In the House of Reptiles,
Behind the safety glass
Of the snake's cage,
Sharing a branch
With its coiled soul mate,
The cricket is singing.

Waiting Out a Storm on a Deserted Farm

The door of this farmhouse
Has fallen out of its frame
Flat on the sunken porch
From threshold to first step,

And the gutters and downspouts
Are giving away their share
Of a cloudburst. The shake roof
Is down on two cornerstones.

One side of the wire fence
Was a garden once; the other,
A pasture full of brambles
And burrs, now come to call

The garden theirs, and roses
Have crawled over and under
The fence to cultivate
The weeds with another wildness.

The man who gave up here
Dug fifty-six postholes
And filled them with quarter-splits
Of unseasoned cottonwood,

Then strung them with two strands
Of No. 2 barbed wire
To hold the lightest touches
Of snow and meadowlarks,

To bear with the full and empty
Talons of saw-whet owls,
And left them there to whistle
In the wind from the North Pole.

But glistening and glinting
Green in the hard rain,
Six of those posts have sprouted
Branches and put out leaves.

Looking into a Crystal Ball

Once you get over seeing even more comic
    Versions of yourself (the prolonged nose,
        The midget brain pan) and the flaws in glass
And your fingerprints and the avenues
    Your sweaty grip left behind, you concentrate
        On deeper matters inside the hemisphere
Bulging toward you. You try to envision
    Something. Do the mists clear? Is there
        Anything worth mentioning or only
The unreflective gloom of this nearly opaque
    Carnival-booth toy that takes in light
        From almost any angle
But the direct point of the perpendicular
    And glances the rest aside beyond your scope
        Like a loss-of-contact lens? All you could ever
Have hoped for or been afraid of—tall dark strangers,
    Money, trips over water, the dangerously
        Familiar incoherent advice of psychic
Readers who go balling around, enjoying
    The snowstorm of your future—you suddenly
        Have them all there, cold, in the palm of your hand.
Now, really, what would you like
    To see in there? And what would you really want
        To hear them whisper?

In the Shade of the Old Apple Tree

There's barely room enough under the branches
    For you to match your spine against the trunk
        Of this old-timer whose carbuncular bark
Is frazzled with loose ends, but it offers you
    Uncompromising support. It doesn't intend
        To give up being here, no matter how
Some suppler and more portable vertebrates
    Prune it and spray it and jab at it with ladders
        And plunder it. Today, what comes between
The two of you isn't just your shirt,
    But a difference of opinion about freehold
        And the natural rights of man. This is November.
Prime apples are long gone into bins and lunch bags
    And, judging by the ferment in the breeze,
        Others have gone to ground
For the homebrewing of worms. What's in the air
    Is a heaviness of intention
        To be done with all this clinging
To fruitful endeavors, to making apples appear
    Out of nowhere, which (just imagine!)
        Turn out to be apples again,
With a green, then yellow-streaked, golden
    Blush-red, crimson, and beyond-
        Empurpled luster. This tree has been dining out
On some of its own windfall for fifty years,
    Has tasted its own taste, and knows its own flavor
        As well as the worms. Among the thinning leaves,
Whose stomata have shut down, not just for the night,
    But for the duration, a few malingerers
        Still hang against the sky. If one were to fall
And land on your head, what form of illumination
    Could you offer in return? That the fruit of the tree
        Isn't necessarily worth peeling

This late in the season? That its impact
    Is less accountable than its calculus?
        Look, one actually falls. It's falling. It fell
And missed you. The stem let go,
    Having done its job and its time, and the apple,
        After bumbling against branches, landed
Hard and soft with a squelch, all pulp and pips
    On the bare earth, where it lies split open,
    Ready for almost anything.

The Book of Moonlight

The Book of Moonlight is not written yet.
—Wallace Stevens

Why should we ever write it? We hold it blank
Under the branches of this hemlock, glowing
And shimmering. Already the light of the moon
Has overflowed its pages and is falling
Across the forest floor where it spells out
The nonsense syllables of the night for us,
Where it murmurs all our names and remembers
The silhouettes of our illiterate fingers.

2

My Father and the Hydrostatic Paradox

Pressure being proportional to depth alone, a very small quantity
of liquid may balance any quantity, however great.
—Lancelot Hogben, *Science for the Citizen*

My father made up his mind that old swamp water
        Wouldn't come up our basement drain again
                In the next hard rain and float
Storage boxes around the laundry tubs
        And rust his tools and douse the furnace grate
                And slosh and scuttle into the coal bin
And just sit there
        For days, a brew of sedges and rotten leaves
                And the bric-a-brac of sewers, a mulch
Of the drowned stuffing of cattails, as slippery
        As Lever Brothers, as oily as Standard Oil,
                Our next-door neighbors. So upright in that drain
He screwed a yard-long gun-metal blue
        Steel pipe and told me the tale of the paradox:
                A half-gallon could stand against Wolf Marsh
And all the cubic miles of Lake Michigan
        If they tried to swamp us again. Through the next rain
                We stood between the wet foot of the stairs
And his muddy workbench, watching the underworld
        Around us climb the inside of that pipe
                An inch a minute up to the foamy brim,
Then quiver and stop, defeated. We celebrated
        By doing a counterclockwise victory strut
                (Since that was the way all North American water
Went down the drain), and while we stomped and smiled,
        Believing in science, those other leagues against us
                Came dribbling, then spurting between the concrete blocks

Of our foundation, spitting out bits of mortar,
Then bubbled up through brand-new cracks in the floor
And slowly refilled our basement. Late the next day
I watched him (braced in hip boots, glum and red
In the face of magic) unscrewing slowly
Counterclockwise the whole clockwise idea.

Speeding

My friends and I wanted to drive fast
Faster to floor the pedal and go roaring
Through stop signs and blind corners our eyes half-stuck
On the needle over the limit throttling the night
While clutching both hands white on the jittery wheel
Or making fists in the backseat seeing the blocks
And blocks of houses streaking by the smear
Of porches out the windshield a lane and a half
Between parked cars an emptiness ready to swallow
Whatever we had to offer beyond the end
Of the engine the grill the chrome-plated star the ram
The streamlined nude thrusting all of us forward
Into the dark past streetlights rushing our way
To vault over our heads and show up again
With nothing new to shine for but another
Cross street another nothing we didn't want
To be somewhere we didn't want to be
Anywhere even sooner than possible
Or somewhere else ahead to be anything
Different something here not now but there
Not then to rocket to break it off
But sooner than we could think we'd see the end
Of the street where going on meant losing it all
So we'd slow down then finally almost maybe
Stopping to talk about how good it had been
Not being afraid of flying past between
Our sleeping mothers and fathers who couldn't see us
Scuffling home now having been somebody
Who would get us through the night and the slow morning
And the slower afternoon the regular walking
Around the sitting the nodding the figuring

And being agreeable dutiful always holding
Close the key the ignition midnight the street
The clear lane revving us up to speed
The same old way our faces and feet were aimed
Our eyes were headed were meant to go by god.

Thinking of What to Say

In that country house where I roomed upstairs
The professor of engineering had forgotten
How to tell anyone what he knew
About statics and the resultants of forces
Because he'd had a cerebral accident
That had interrupted the flow
Of his conversation. He was learning
To say his words again, thanks to his patient
Loving wife. Whenever we met,
He would look at me and smile till his eyes watered,
Remembering how to say, *How
Are you?* but forgetting what came after
Besides *Good-bye* and the rigid tip of his tongue
Which must have felt by then like the tip
Of an iceberg. I watched my mouth
In the mirror, wondering what I would do
If words became that hard to find at the end
Of my tongue or fingers and what I might make
Out of the words of others worth the rest
Of my time to myself. I sat there in my room
Grading tongue-tied freshman decompositions
By the hour and the foot-pound
While out the window the leaf-covered lawn
Swept down invitingly to a country club
I could barely imagine playing. One afternoon
As I parked my rattling Ford in the driveway,
Two serious young men in narrow suits,
As late in their twenties as I was, stood between
Me and my rented door and said they were asking
That I not use my room until evening,
That the President of the United States
Was going to play golf outside my window
And would rather I didn't watch him doing it.

I had been going to brood about a poem
And maybe go so far
As to put something or other on a page
While sitting beside myself beside that window.
I had found it helped to look at the real world
While saying anything, however lame,
About the other worlds I was beginning
To scratch and claw and wriggle my way through.
I didn't want to be president.
I hardly even wanted to be myself.
I had killed a sparrow once with a BB gun
Before I could think
And had suffered then almost as vividly
As I still suffer remembering
How I did it. I opened my mouth
To tell the Secret Service I wouldn't dream
Of shooting around or through Dwight Eisenhower
And wouldn't know what to say
About seeing him choose a club or address his ball
Through the window on the only visible hole—
A par four with a fairway trap
And a dogleg where he might take a chance
Of laying up and hitting a long three-wood
Across the rough. But nothing came out
From between my lips, not even my cold tongue,
So I backed down the drive and, like the leader
Of the Western world, who also had problems
Reading his papers and thinking what to say next
Or in the first place, whiled away the hours
Till supper and sundown at a loss for words.

For a Mockingbird

Oaxaca, Mexico

In the market, all were for sale:
In cages hung on wires
Canaries and wild finches
Were hopping, chirping, and warbling,

Now seeing their shut lids
More clearly than the sky,
Having forgotten where
And what and why they were.

But from a cage the size
Of a trap, a mockingbird
Stared at me, not moving,
Half-crouched, alert, silent.

His beautifully slender
Pointed and curved beak
Was closed. He had been waiting.
He had forgotten nothing.

I made him mine by the law
Of the market and my pocket
And carried his cramped cell
To a garden by my hotel.

I lifted his roof away.
He waited a long moment,
Then fluttered out and flew
Over bricks cracked by the sun

To the cross-brace of an awning,
To the arched bridge of a trellis
And clung there, motionless,
Crouching among roses

With his round unwavering
Eye still fixed on mine.
What was he waiting for?
Had I forgotten something?

They can mimic every sound
They hear except for words
And thunder, we're told. They remember
Everything they admire

And make it part of their song,
Not mockingly, but truly.
I whistled three times, lamely.
His thin black beak stayed shut.

He sailed to a gold branch
By a wall, waited and stared
Again at me, then sailed
Over it and was gone.

In a Country Cemetery

I had been reading tombstones and drinking in
    Their verses with my beer—the heavenly comforts
        In heavenly homes and the folly
Of earthly pleasures. I thought I had been
    Thoughtful while putting my feet down
        Among resting places, knee-high in timothy,
Going from plot to plot, avoiding
    The plastic flowers and daffodils
        Still in their jam jars. I had touched
The names and the odd numbers of men,
    Women, and infants who had been lying there
        So long, the who's and when's of what they'd been
Were flaking away to nothing. I was taking them
    And myself as seriously as my six-pack,
        Had memorized epitaphs
With every bottle, had counted on them,
    Had given them the attention we deserved,
        Had given them pride of place
In my mind and stomach, and felt well
    Under their influence. The final drafts,
        Now grown nearly as warm as I was,
Had rendered me fully capable
    Of understanding the positions of these companions
        Composed of earth, truly composed
At last, so I lay down among them
    To share their gray-blue afternoon, their words
        And mine intermingled. I had just begun
To know the stretches of heaven
    That appeared and reappeared and disappeared
        Between my eyelids and the even stiffer
Stretches of firmament
    Under me, when a voice—as distinct from the wind
        As lightning from dim daylight—called me

From the barely audible edge
    Of silence. *Daaavid. Daaaaavid.* It spoke
        To the back of my mind or the bottom
Or whatever part of it was still willing
    And able to listen, and though I didn't think
        This was the Voice That Breathed O'er Eden
Or the judgment call of Gabriel, that name
    Came all the way from my dead mother and father
        And my dream children, all the way
From the brim of the untranslatable, unknown
    Tongue of love, and bewildered, I gathered
        The little that seemed left
Of my spilled body and stood it up
    And blundered it to the brow of a long slope
        Downhill and heard again
In a woman's voice the name of that dead poet
    From a farm on the lower field. She wanted someone
        Far away, but not so far
He couldn't be called back. She needed him
    And expected him to hear her.
        She wanted him to come home now,
Please, maybe to do something
    Important for her, because it was getting late,
        Before it was too late.

Wild Cucumber

The tall, wide sheriff's deputy wanted to know
What I was doing, walking along barbed wire
In my old clothes and boots beside a swamp,
My car parked in the mud at a farmer's gate
And the fog that morning still light in the fields.

He said he'd been watching me from a distance.
He'd seen me use my field glasses and notebook
As if I might be waiting for someone.
He said he was sorry, but they liked to be sure
Who was who this close to the Honor Farm.

He hoped I'd understand he was obliged
To find out who I was. He needed to place me.
I showed him my permission to drive a car
And told him my occupations. From under his Stetson
He looked at our mutual swamp suspiciously.

Then leaning against a fence post overgrown
By wild cucumber, he said some prisoners
Have very fancy plans about getting away,
And he didn't think it was a good idea
For me to be walking here. He said some people

Might get the wrong impression. He'd rather see me
Somewhere I belonged. While I backed out
And realigned myself on that country road,
He picked a cucumber and began to peel it
Absentmindedly with his bare hands.

I could have told him: under his jackboots,
Sprawled halfway down that embankment somewhere short
Of swampwater, Manroot, *marah oreganus,*
A root the size of a man, as thick and long
As a deputy, was hiding underground.

I could have told him it had brought to life,
As it did each spring, a burst of drab, ragged,
Open-ended flowerheads and out of a tangle
Of cling-tights, hooks, and spurs had ripened them
To inedible, spiny, jagged, hard-cased, raspy,

Burr-like, runt cucumbers. It was lying
Doggo now, underfoot, in perfect concealment,
Producing a mockery of fruit nobody wanted,
Having escaped forever. Still watching me,
He made a flip *So long* with bleeding fingers.

The Path

The path led just a shade too steeply
    Down to a mountain lake, and if you walked it
        Cautiously by daylight
In a dry season, you could keep
    Your feet under you all the way
        To the dockside, the mossy steps,
And the rowboat, where you could stand
    Reflecting under the cedars and imagine,
        Afloat or sinking, your life all over
Again. As a young bride,
    My grandmother-in-law had named it
        Lake Byron, had rowed herself
To the deepest part and dropped a *Collected Byron*
    Over the side as a promise
        Of Romance. In later years, some poets
Visited her in her absence
    On separate occasions and had much in common
        Though not with her: they felt
Romantically inclined to stroll
    Without their spouses before sleep near midnight
        To examine broken moonlight
Or light rain on the water,
    And on the path, they braced their shoes
        Along the fish-boned crevices
In the clay, and all of them,
    To a man, having great faith
        In their own goat-footedness
And natural balance stepped lightly
    And gallantly into the gloom and went sliding
        Down in a smooth pratfall. James Wright
And Richard Hugo, James Dickey, Theodore Roethke—
    All, without exception, not having spilled
        A single drop of their drinks, reordered

Their mud-streaked slacks and laughed
     At themselves, stood up, and slithered
          With ingenious, individually inventive
Dignified footwork, pivoting, fishtailing
     To an end-stop at the water's edge, where each gave
          A toast to the resident owl, the moon,
And Lord Byron. Each one stood
     On the swaying planks, each braced
          Himself, hunched, half-squatted,
Opened his mouth wide, and interrupted
     With serious rough *basso buffo*
          Reverberant joy the croaks
Of the bullfrogs. They all listened
     Respectfully and hopefully
          To the sudden silence,
Which was the frogs' invariable answer, then turned
     And with their empty glasses began climbing
          Resignedly back uphill.

Keeping Quiet at the Benedictine Abbey

I was going down to breakfast after a night
    Of being so quiet I could hear myself
        Listening to myself. I slouched along
A corridor whose right wall suddenly turned
    To glass through which, as if in a lineup mirror,
        I could see brothers
In floor-length robes, a single-file procession
    Marching buoyantly next to me, smiling ahead
        As if the night behind us had been so full
Of happiness, they were only leaving it
    Because it led to an even greater kind
        Of oatmeal and bread without the benefit
Of butter or jelly. To be a Benedictine
    Is to be under orders not to laugh
        At anything, not even the likes of me,
And not a solitary, single young man
    Looked my way along his homespun cowl,
        Either from some holy preoccupation
Or from a sure and certain hope of not
    Breaking up at the sight of my baggy slacks
        And sweatshirt, the barely permissible treason
Of a clerk. They had all been sworn to speak
    Well of the world as soon as they were given
        Permission to speak again. Meanwhile, we played
The other part: we curved our lower lips
    Against the corners of our stiff upper lips
        And kept our own counsel. What exactly
They got out of this, besides a more relaxed
    Voice box and a flaccid epiglottis,
        No doubt they've learned in time. Perhaps they became
Good listeners to the plaints of visiting poets
    Who spoke some ill of the world, made joyful noises,
        Then suffered the guilt of special ham and eggs.

At the Ruins of Baalbek, 1971

She saw me coming out of the dusty taxi
    And across the lot by the ruins of Baalbek,
        And her whole body rippled
As if to say, *Another!* She was wearing
    Her orange-and-indigo-tufted finery,
        Her sequined bridle, and a high back-bracing
Wooden saddle between her bedraggled humps
    For the next tourists who wanted to look at themselves
        Later, shifting shapes like their own mirages
Onboard a ship of the desert. While her driver
    Prodded her down to her knees (front first), she groaned
        And puffed, then shut her nostrils
At the indignity of having to go through this
    Again for an unbeliever. Her hind legs hunched
        And dropped their burden down into a huddle,
But her language said she wanted no part of me
    On her back. As I straddled her
        Warily, she reassembled her joints, reared up
At the rear, and sent me bowing against my knees,
    Braced all her toes, and lifted both of us
        So far off the ground, the Roman rubble
Shrank into postcards. Pillars and capitals
    Lost their jammed perspectives. She was glancing
        Sideways at me, batting her sand-proof lashes,
Pursing her lips, deciding which was more
    To her taste: spitting or biting. I tried to smile
        As she yawed and billowed and gave me a little something
To remember her by—a camera flash and a rattle
    From the stomach at the end of her Chain of Being—
        Then took two steps (for both of us,
The first and last legs of a journey to nowhere)
    And sank deliberately from fore to aft
        Back to the earth and rested there

On undisputed ground. When I'd been dismounted,
      I could almost imagine I knew I could believe
            She had been someone's joy, the savior
Of her tribe, the mother of gentle warriors,
      The gift of Allah, her unlikely body
            An oasis of food and shelter, but now the flies
In their hundreds had regathered
      At her cracked and bleeding calluses, at the corners
            Of the shriveled worlds of her eyes,
And unable to change my mind
      About anything, I taxied off through the shade
            Of the lost cedars of Lebanon, on the road
Away from Damascus, where hooded Bedouins
      Hunched over melons the size of hand grenades,
            Toward a tall city surrounded by lost tribes.

Elegy on the First Day of Spring

In my mother's garden even the ragweed
    Struggled for life. The plants I sent her
        Bloomed, then wilted and withered
And died in the sandy soil through the hard summers
And even harder winters. She died
        In a nursing home, having forgotten
Who she was, her father and mother, her husband,
    Her three bewilderingly distant children,
        The names of almost everything
Around her, her whole life. But she could sing.
    She could still be seated carefully at the piano
        In her flowered housecoat and play
And sing for hours the music she'd memorized
    When she was a girl. She played while other ladies
        And gentlemen in easy chairs or wheelchairs
Listened or sang along or slept. *The Flower*
    That Once Has Bloomed, Le Givre
        En Fleur, Du bis wie eine Blume
In her soft clear barely
    Audible soprano. I wanted to be something
        Like her flower once, thinking
I might be one
    Of the few that would survive
        More than one winter, so I came to live
In a place where gardens thrive. On this first day
    Of spring, in spite of me, my garden is ready
        To break into blossom. I have to make room
For everything, uproot and cut, thin out,
    Transplant and reorder. But instead, I'm making
        A place for these words among different weeds

In a time for recalling everything.
The earth wants to make music. The sun
Is coming our way again
With everything it had forgotten, opening itself
And us again, as astonished as we are
At everything we can still remember.

Our Hands

Hands off, I say to my daughters, and *Keep your hands*
    To yourselves. They can smudge
        Almost anything reachable, though they've learned
How not to knock over glasses or drop spoons
    Or cookies or grapes, how not to put their fingers
        Into their cereal. But they grip pencils
Boldly and swirl to the end and off
    The paper onto the table and take a firm hand
        With everything they covet, pinching,
Pummeling, scratching, yet can suddenly turn
    Their fists into private holdings
        So soft and small that when those refuges
Uncurl, you wouldn't want to call them empty.
    But my own are even more disorderly
        And unpredictable. I keep them
To myself too often. My daughters ask to see one
    Now, and we look together. I know my palm
        Like the back of my hand: the long lines
Of the Heart and Restlessness
    And Life, the shorter lines of the Head
        And Marriage, the almost nonexistent
Line of Intuition, Solomon's
    Broken Ring, the impassable Mount of Venus.
        When characters stare
At their hands on stage, they mean, *What have I done?*
    What should I do? But these two girls
        Stare at mine, not to find out
What they may amount to or whether I've washed them
    Lately or bitten them to the quick
        Or whether they've fumbled away

What they most value: they think I'm hiding
    Something important, some wonderful
        Surprise! Half-smiling, they wait
For their good fortune. It's up my sleeve
    Or in my pocket instead. Or invisible.
        And they only have to be quiet long enough
For it to appear like magic. What could it be?
    If only my fixed lines were more like theirs:
        Still faint, still tentative, the creases seeming
Momentary ripples in linen
    To be shaken smooth in the morning
        And made ready for night.

The End of the Story

After dressing up out of a dress-up basket
As mermaids and flappers, babysitters and androids,
Teachers and firefighters and their own mother,
The two girls in pajamas are on the sofa
On each side of their father, bare feet dangling,
Waiting to listen to this fairy tale
For the first time. They hear how a baby
Lives in a castle with the King and Queen
And has a birthday party, how a bad fairy
Puts a curse on the baby who grows up
To be a Princess while her worried daddy
Banishes every spindle from his kingdom.
(They know *spindle*'s a word for something you want
But you can't have it. They gather the hard facts
And stretch their toes and lean in from both sides.)
And when the Princess snoops upstairs in the wrong
Part of the castle and finds a bad old lady
With a bad spindle, they're not in the least surprised.
It's what a princess *would* do. She *needed* one,
And if she could possibly prick her finger with it,
Of course she would. But now she's falling asleep.
Instantly. Plop. They both sit still,
Amazed by that. Their eyes are turning
White from corner to corner, trying to catch
Themselves falling asleep. They imagine the castle
Falling asleep, how everyone cooking the food
In the kitchen falls asleep, how the dogs and cats
And the mice and houseflies all at once decide
To fall asleep, how the mouths of the King and Queen
Sag open and snore. They straighten up for the Prince
And listen to him scraping through the roses
And follow him, step by step, through dusty hallways

And up the staircase to the cobwebby room
Where they lie waiting for him, having no idea
He's coming closer and closer and being struck
Dumb by how beautiful they are. They have no notion
He's bending over them and puckering
And being so daring as to kiss them, smack,
And suddenly they waken, astonished, not by the King
And Queen and the household and the animals
And the insects and the kitchen fire, all springing
Back to life, but by this joy of jumping
Around and kissing the backs of their hands and the air
And each other and their groggy mother and father
Who tell them now they have to fall asleep
And wake up later in a different story.

Alexandra and the Thunder

Seven-year-old Alexandra has cried out
Loud in the night because something has come through
The ceiling and crammed itself against her walls
And her floor and battered the air
With a six-sided barrage of what she knows
Is supposed to be called *thunder.* She's lying rigid
On her back. She doesn't like it. *Tell me
Again,* she says, *what does that?* I say lightning.
A bunch of electricity far away
Goes from one place to another, a big jolt
Goes boom way off on the other side of the hills
Or up in the mountains, and what you hear
Is the noise come rolling and rumbling all these miles
Over the trees and through the rain to our house.

I don't like it to do that, she says. *It shakes me.*
It shakes everybody, not just you.
Are you sure it's the lightning? Yes, I say. *All right.*

I stand in her doorway, seeing blurrily
The blurred outlines of her menagerie,
The flock on the quilt guarding their shepherdess
Through the darkness, members of nearly every known
And unknown species, even the shorn lamb
For whom God is supposed to temper the wind.
And a flash suddenly half-illuminates
My sagging eyelids, and five or so seconds later
The whole partnership of the house and roof
And its timbers shudders and shakes on the foundation.

I wait for her frightened call out of the shadows.
She says nothing. She's gone to sleep, apparently
Having believed me. I sidle back to my share
Of the innersprings of the night and try to believe
Myself, to forget, to remember what thunder
Is. *Baffle-gloom-numb-dumb-tomb-bloody-humdrum-doom,*
It mumbles, shaking both of us.

Dancing Daughters

It comes as naturally to them as standing up
In the morning or lying down at night. My daughters
Want to dance all day, and they don't care
Whether the samba or frug or macarena
Is the thrill of the moment or whether the hanky-panky
Includes a grande jeté. They're head over heels
For a ring around the farmer in the dell
Or a space-cake walk. They want to go over
And under the limbo stick at the same time.

But their dance-deprived daddy's single gift in the Land
Of Terpsichore is a kind of work-release polka.
He can only show them the living memorial
Of a foxtrot, how to nestle each right hand
In his left, to accept his other under their wings
And tame their toes to his slowly shuffling feet
On the carpet while he croons over their heads,
I can't give you anything but love,
Baby, but something else is snapping their fingers
And saying *Let's get moving.* They can remember
Only an hour ago they jumped and boogied
At the mere idea of going to Grandma's,
And their feet remember vaulting, their skinny hips
Remember going sideways and widdershins,
They know their knees can rattle sockets, their shoulders
Tip them down and around like melting witches,
They want to dance with the dog, to go dancing in
And out of restaurants and ladies' rooms
And up and down the aisles of groceries. Oh,
They want to dance in the bathtub. They want to wiggle
While brushing their teeth, while yawning, while taking off
Their panties and finding the wide ends of their nightgowns
And when, just for a while, they finally
Go flat, they do it only as long as they can
Go on dreaming of heeling and toeing it
Just a little bit longer under the covers.

Night Light

The two girls want to know
    (When they open their eyes
In the night) the shapes between them
    And their doors are still
Where they were or they'll think
    They're both back there
In the dark of their dreams where ogres
    And witches snort and cackle
And make mistakes and where good girls
    Can't always get away
Fast enough. When their eyelids
    Open, they want to see something
Easier to get along with
    Than darkness. I try to tell them
Darkness is beautiful,
    And they can be even darker
And still be sure
    To find themselves. They can feel
At home without luminous patches
    Glowing against the wall
Like nests of fireflies
    And they don't have to feel
Trapped under the covers, wondering
    Where in the world they are
And where they're going
    To be if it's ever morning
Again, and I say why don't they
    Rise up and sing or dance
Downstairs or run outdoors
    In the back of their minds
On their pillows? But if they hear
    Something strange and can't see it,

They feel afraid. I say their daylight teachers
    Have told them about bats
Who chirp and chitter all night and know
    Where almost everything is
And about owls who can sleep
    With one of their big old eyes
Open. I promise them their own
    Big eyes and ears can be as sure
As bats' and owls' in the dark,
    And while they lie there, thinking
Of answers, I say good night
    And plug in the night-light.

In the Snow

On a sunless moonless evening
Along an empty highway
He was running in the snow
Barefoot and ankle-deep,
Putting each foot down
Heavily, steadily,
And I was running beside him,
Wanting to ask him where
We were going, whether someone
Was chasing us, whether we were
Chasing ourselves home
Again or running away,
But he wouldn't look at me.
The set of his jaw, the tilt
And heft of his thick shoulders
Meant he was only running
Because he was supposed to.
He said nothing, and I saw
Our car ahead of us
In the ruts of the embankment.
He ran to the open door
And slumped in the backseat.
I slid behind the wheel
And sat there shivering,
Waiting, catching my breath,
Wondering who had the key,
My father breathless behind me.

3

Thoreau and the Stumps

Farmers along the river found no profit
    In stumps, those plow-breakers. They shoveled
        The dirt from under them and chained them
To mules or oxen, strained and hacked
    Till the last of the roots gave way, then hauled them
        Off to the edge of the woods
By the riverbank like bony demons
    To be left for dead. And there Thoreau would choose
        One, would hitch his ropes, and drag it slowly
Downslope, having to joggle and lurch,
    Push, unsnag it, and drag again
        And struggle it into the stern of his rowboat
And get it seated with its ungainly legs
    Stretched skyward and stiffened over the gunwales,
        And row that hulking passenger toward home,
Where he would have to lumber it to his woodyard
    And settle it beside more orderly firewood,
        A misshapen presence, hardheaded
And stubborn. With wedge and maul, with ax
    And bucksaw, he would split and chop at the base,
        At the involuted, knotted, almost unbreakable
Mass of the heartroot and wrench loose,
    A few at a time, crookshank, elbow, and twist,
        And savor them in his fire, crosshatched,
At odds with each other, and likely to fidget
    Apart as if not fit for any posture
        But their own. They would snap
And shimmer into flame and then glare
    And hiss, sputter and redden
        Like iron at the mouth of the smith's bellows
But instead of melting would gradually
    Shrink into a near-whiteness that would hover
        At the backs of his eyes, shut

Or open in the afterglow. He could remember,
He told himself, the shape of every root
As it took its place in his fire, the earth
Still clinging tight as if one fed the other
To the end while both turned luminous
To cast their light over his scrawled pages.

Thoreau and the Body

The lighthouse-keeper told him where he could find it,
    So feeling duty-bound to survey
        What he'd never seen before, he began walking
For miles along the cold November beach
    At the rim of the surf where every moment
        The spent waves would thin at his feet and pause
And go back to their source
    And return for another moment, and at last
        He saw it from far off, half-buried,
Lying aslant in the dry, wind-trampled sand,
    And he approached it soberly, circumspectly,
        Like a distant relative at a memorial—
The remains of a human being
    Cast up by the sea. He felt
        Pleasantly surprised by the coherence
Of backbone and ribcage and and was impressed
    By how inoffensive the frayed ribbons of flesh
        And tissue had been rendered
By the efforts of sharks and starfish, the ministrations
    Of crabs and the attendant orders
        Of shrimps and plankton. He was much taken
By the open-mindedness of the skull,
    Its frank disclosures, its willingness to share
        Eccentric points of view. Here lay
A mortal treasury to be dispersed
    In an exchange of gifts among kingdoms.
        Although the phenomenal world—the waves, the tide,
The shore, and the air itself—was hanging
    In suspense around the body of this death,
        The event demanded nothing from an observer
But a passage of cold attention, then a more
    Extended forgetfulness. Refreshed, reassured,
        He walked away to forget.

Thoreau and the Crickets

He found them bedded in ice, in the frozen puddles
        Among reeds and clumps of sedges in the marsh:
                House and field crickets lying near the surface
On their sides or upside down, their brittle hind legs
        Cocked as if to jump as free as fiddlers
                In the final rain before winter. The ice
Had clarified the brown and green shades
        Of their chitin and magnified
                The thickened radiant veins of the forewings
On which they'd made their music
        Those nights when he'd listened, half-asleep,
                To their creaking, their wise old saws
That told him over and over they were with him
        And of him down to the vibrant depths
                Of his eardrums and canals and the foundation
Of his house on earth. With his heels and hands
        He broke the puddles around them carefully,
                Cracking them loose and filling his coat pockets
With fragments like clear glass, holding them hard
        As fossils in shale. He would take them home
                And learn from them, examine their lost lives
With scales and ruler, tweezers and microscope.
        He would bring them back to order and pay homage
                To all they'd been and left undone. He strode
Briskly and happily through the crusted lanes
        And slipped through the paths of town, delighted
                To be alive all winter, to be ready
And able to warm their spirits with his own,
        But on his doorstep, reaching into his coat,
                He lifted out, dripping with snow-melt,
Two hands full of wriggling, resurrected crickets
        Crawling over each other, waving and flexing
                Antennae and stiff legs to search his palms

For another springtime. For a while, he held them
  And watched them wriggle drunkenly
    And scrabble in half-death for what they imagined
He had to give, then put them gently
  Again into his pockets and carried them
    Back through the snow and ice to their cold beds.

Thoreau and the Toads

After the spring thaw, their voices ringing
    At dusk would beckon him through the meadow
        To the edge of their pond where, barefoot,
He would wade slowly into the water
    And stand there in the last of light
        To see the mating toads—a hundred or more
In the shallows around him, ignoring him
    Or taking him for another, inflating
        The pale-green bubbles of their throats to call
For *buffo terrestris,* leaping half out of the pool
    And scrambling to find partners. The atmosphere
        Would quiver with their harmonic over-
And undertones, with their loud, decent proposals
    Like the sounds of a church potluck, their invocations
        And offertories for disorderly conduct,
With the publishing of their indelicate banns
    And blessings to the needy in their distress
        And benedictions even beyond springtime
To all those of the faith. And he would see
    Among this communal rapture, there underwater,
        The small gray males lying silent
On the backs of females, holding on
    To their counterparts with every slippery finger
        And toe, both motionless, both gazing
Inward at the Indivisible
    And rising from time to time together
        To the surface only an inch above them
To breathe, then settling again and staring
    With such a consciousness of being
        Common American toads, he would stand beside them,
As content as they were with their medium
    Of exchange, the soles of his feet trembling
        With a resonance he could feel deep in his spine,

Believing this mud could be his altar too,
     And his pulpit, where all of his intentions
          Would be as clear as theirs, as clear as the air
In the chill of the fading light. He would lift
     His bare feet gently and silently, making scarcely
          A ripple, balancing
Himself onto the grass and, while his brethren
     Like a drunken choir went on
          And on without him, would sit down
Vibrant on the earth and once again struggle
     Into his stockings, into his waterproof boots,
          And straighten and square-knot his rawhide laces.

Thoreau and the Catfish

While he was wading in the swamp knee-deep
    He saw underwater a hole in the muddy bank
        As wide as his hand, and for no more reason
Than his own right hand could tell him, he crouched down
    And reached in slowly
        Up to the wrist and along his forearm
Inch by inch into that softness
    And gradually deeper through a passageway
        Into what seemed an opening-out, a chamber,
And there in that yielding room
    With the very ends of his fingertips, he felt
        One after another something
Like the roots of target weeds allowing themselves
    To be brushed aside, but then, as if in answer,
        Returning to him. The right eye
In his tilted head was almost touching
    The ripples of the pond, and the other
        Blinked at the sky, but all his life
Quivered inside his fingers as they closed
    Gently and grappled firmly, bringing along
        And down with them and out through the darkness
And up into the air (as he stood upright
    To stare into her streaming, dripping face)
        A foot-long catfish, whose barbels swayed
On all sides of her snout. She was not thrashing
    Or clamping the bristling rows
        Of gristle on her upper jaw as he held her
In suspense, as dark as the matter
    Falling along her sides in rivulets
        Like candle wax and dripping onto his arm
And under it. Her sunken eyes
    Reflected nearly nothing. He was gazing
        Deep into the mother who was still

In her own dream, not shaking
        In his hand. Her translucent fins
            And her barbels all seemed imperturbable
As he lowered her again into the water,
        And found the mouth of the passage and carefully
            Replaced her in her nest and left her there,
And his whole arm came back to him once more
        To be beside him under its own power,
            Its skin as black as hers.

Thoreau Wading in a River

On summer days at the swampy edge of the river
    He would bundle his shirt and shoes, his pantaloons
        And drawers on the dry bank
And wearing only a wide-brimmed hat
    Would begin his water walk, light-footed,
        Feeling his way as deliberately
As a heron, at first upstream, even more slowly
    Than the slow current against him, and with one hand
        Would touch the lives of bedstraw and water starwort,
The open mouths of sundew, the radical leaves
    Of floating heart, dull claret and green,
        Pellucid in tufts and fringed
Like carrageen moss—all waders and waverers
    That had learned to take the earth like him as it came
        And went with the swells and fallings-away
Of wavelets and backwash. And at noon he would turn
    And retrace his morning, sinking gradually
        Deeper, seeing his feet like the undersides
Of flatfish taking their places calmly, surrounded
    And then overcome by the dark debris and algae
        Of the bottom, leaf mold, the empty houses
Of frog spawn, the casings of caddis larvae,
    Among the castaway sheaths of ephemerella,
        Of stoneflies, the husks of pondweeds melting
Under them, up through shallows a foot deep,
    That would suddenly shelve and soften
        Down into valleys till the surface rose
To circle his bare neck (the water as warm
    As he was and as given to change), then to fall
        To his breast, to his midriff, rippled
By all the piecemeal reflections
    The sun could cast through branches, the fragments
        Of its commentary on the passing order,

And through it, beyond it, midway
    At his knees, the suspended blur of being
      Held there, amiable as death, the wheeling
Cilia of rotifers in the living dust,
    And see his body rise
      As the bed rose to a surface thinning to nothing
And feel himself shedding the skin of the river,
    Ready to wear again, as his own man,
      The bundle of dry clothes there on the shore.

Thoreau and the Cow

He was walking home through a meadow, all his senses
    Alert to recognize and remember
        Everything, when he came to a slow pause
Among cows, noticing one, a heavy matron
    Standing motionless, staring upward. The others
        In the small herd had all lowered their heads
To browse, to engage their already engorged
    Milk sacs, or were dozing on the level,
        Chewing once more the green slush in their cuds,
But she had lifted her underjaw and wattle
    And with wide-open eyes was staring at the sky,
        And he stopped dead to drink her in.
He'd never seen a cow gaze at the heavens.
    When he followed her example, there seemed to be
        Nothing where she was looking—a few light clouds,
The ordinary vacancy at the end
    Of a day without weather. He stood and watched.
        Whatever she was seeing meant more to her
Than the stems of purslane dangling from one corner
    Of her shut mouth, suspended as if forever
        Between her mandibles and their fulfillment.
He thought he had understood all of this meadow
    As well as the next cow or the next field mouse
        From the ice of the first season
To the fire of the last, had floated on it
    In spring floods, had bathed among snapping turtles
        Before official summer, had waded
In gum boots along paths of his own invention,
    And now he could hardly believe
        There was anything in the sky or underfoot
He hadn't named, not even the filaments
    Of gossamer spiders aloft on their one journey,
        But there she was, transfixed

By what he couldn't see. He waited with her
        In case the God of Cows might make Himself
        Manifest to an innocent bystander,
Then trudged on home, too puzzled and disappointed
    And embarrassed to hope for what he saw in her:
        The aura of adoration.

4

In the Experimental Pool

The students didn't have to do anything
    But lie there in the pool
        And be paid well by the hour
For nothing, to give in to the idea
    Of nothing, with earplugs and sealed eyes,
        With tubes for feeding and waste
And a third for breathing. They were asked to float
    In body-temperature water, to enjoy
        Themselves, to think, to take it easy,
To draw their own conclusions
    About time and light, about lightness
        And heaviness, noise and silence, about touching
Or being touched. They only had to be
    There and not make waves and be paid for as long
        As they felt all right about it,
So they did it: they settled down
    And allowed themselves to be held
        In a perfect Here and Now. At first they planned
Schedules of days and weeks, drew calendars
    In their minds' eyes, rearranged
        And perfected programs, outlines of time and space,
And then they began to remember on purpose
    Whatever they could remember, taking pleasure
        In everything they could recall, the songs
They'd learned by heart, jingles, and nursery rhymes
    They'd only half-forgotten. They played old games
        With words, invented new games that slowly grew
Too intricate to remember. They recollected
    People they'd known and lost, and all the people
        They'd failed to become, and then they struggled
To leave those scenes behind
    By falling asleep, but found they didn't believe
        They'd been asleep when they wakened

To the same absolute darkness. They had more leisure
        Than they'd ever known or found
            Imaginable and felt as full
Of themselves as their warm floating skins
        Would allow. And always somewhere
            Between the second night and the first day
Or the evening of the first or third afternoon,
        The nightmares would begin. They'd realize
They held in their right hands
        A simple switch to tell the invisible man
            On the edge of the pool (who was waiting for them
To do what they were bound to do) they no longer
        Wanted to be paid to lie in the water,
            And all would be lifted out and have their eyes
Opened, and their ears, and be allowed
        To touch their world again and taste it,
            To stand on it and balance their whole weight
In one direction and walk away in another,
        And for days after, someone they didn't know
            Would walk beside them, someone still floating
And dreaming, who wouldn't be told
        Not to follow them everywhere, who would sit
            Beside them at lunch and dinner, who crowded them
In private and listened to everything they could say,
        Who opened the locked doors of their bedrooms,
            Who climbed into bed with them and said good night.

Symposium

The professor of comparative literature
Is lying in the hallway this afternoon
Between the stairwell and a locked glass-case,
Not quite blocking the entrance to the mail room.
Though his hair is still combed neatly, his houndstooth jacket
Appears to have grown too small for his upper torso,
And his dark slacks have shortened above his ankles,
Exposing inappropriate blue socks
With brown suede shoes. A stack of bound term papers
Lies next to him in their original order.

A quiet, attentive group of graduate students
And faculty has gathered loosely around him
While a campus policeman kneels and turns him over.
Behind the lenses of his wire-rimmed glasses
His eyes are firmly closed. His mouth is a slit.
His large square face has brightened
To the inexpressive ruddiness of greasepaint.

He wears a mask of mucus from nose to chin.
The policeman covers it with plastic film,
But before he's mouth-to-mouth, the professor's lips
Sink inward with the raw irregular snore
Of Cheyne-Stokes respiration, a farewell rattle.

His dignity has seldom been so apparent:
His power to cause reflection, to persuade,
To influence and enrich the lives of others,
To deepen their understanding, to arouse
An empathetic tremor in his listeners
Who begin discussing the mordant implications
Of his presentation, the likely interconnections
With other disciplines, and his shades of meaning.

But now the collapsible gurney is lifting him
Out of context, is rolling him out the door
And down the walkway into the ambulance
And driving him beyond their frames of reference.

Dead Letter from Out of Town

When I feel a Northwest town may trigger a poem, before I start writing I assume one or more of the following—. . . David Wagoner has seen the town, assessed it realistically, and decided it is a good place to steer clear of.
—Richard Hugo, *The Triggering Town*

Dick, you were right. I steered clear of that town.
The river that runs through it is as stagnant
As a drainage ditch, the weather an amalgam
Of mildewed paper, slush, dead steam, and phlegm.
The only tavern's built out of used firebrick
And looks like a walk-in safe. The sweet young thing
On the barstool nursing a cooler may have something
But it's in her purse and loaded. The jukebox is broken.
The nearest emergency ward is a trapdoor
In the john—one-way to Ashland. The dork who looks good
For an afternoon of heartbreaking bullshit
Has a badge in his wallet and specializes in busting
Down-on-their-luck nomads who laugh too much.
The card room doubles as the jail: no pens,
No paper, no TV. All games are called
On account of darkness. It's No Smoking forever.
And the girls you might have made, who might have danced
Your way all night and made you feel light-footed?
One lies half-buried in a vacant lot,
Another's caught on a snag in the reservoir,
And the prettiest one, the one voted most likely
To get out of town in time to be somebody,
Is sprouting flowerless plants in a crawl space.
Don't go, old friend. It pulls the trigger once.

Howl

Startled at first, you think something
        Is being killed. Some poor maimed creature
                Needs help in the night, and all this yelping
Is a last stab before it forgets how
        To make any noise at all. You hear it
                And you want to run out the door into the darkness
With a flashlight and give first aid
        Or the comfort of quick burial,
                But before you're out of bed, almost before
You're out of your easy sleep, the coyote raises
        The level of its discourse, the acute angle
                Of its muzzle and lower jaw and pours forth
The beginning of a deeply annoying solo
        Of distress, immediately answered
                And given a skewed dimension by another
From farther out on the prairie, the third and fourth
        Voices flatly and sharply fugal, singing,
                We thought we were going to die today
But didn't. And listen: we won't. This is exactly
        How it sounds to die
                But we don't. So isn't it wonderful
To make any kind of music? We're promising
        The best voices and minds of our generation
                Will thrive and make their marks, then howl for the next.

The Son of a Glover

A note for the biographers of Shakespeare

Because the skin of his fingers had touched the skins
    Of fawns and lambs and kids so often before
        And after his father's knives and shears
Had done their work, he would prefer
    Not wearing gloves at all, even in winter.
        He would see the gloves on other hands as masks
For feelings, with a peculiar understanding
    Of their cost, and would listen
        With an impatience hard to master
To uninformed opinions of light leather,
    Its care and keeping. He would glance
        At his naked palms with so calm a satisfaction
That strangers, even close friends, might mistake the cast
    Of his face for self-regard. Too often,
        He would keep his hands to himself.

The Loneliness of the 100-Meter Dash Man

Crouching, he puts the stiffened tips of his fingers
    Down on the starting line and braces
        The cleats under his toes
Against the springboards
    Of starting-blocks and begins
        Listening hard
To the Ready, the Get Set,
    And the first tremor
        From his eardrums through both hammers and anvils
To the ganglions of his conglomerate
    Skeleton and its collateral
        Balancing rods and pinions for the explosion
Of their propellants blurring him into motion,
    The clenched fists becoming fins, everything
        Joining now to carry the skull and torso
Directly forward to where he wants to go
    (Which is obvious) as quickly and evenly
        As is humanly possible, and almost instantly
He's bowing to the horizontal tape
    Which breaks and falls. It was there
        All along, the limit of every gesture
He wanted to make, and it's gone, flying
    Aside as if it might as well be
        Lying on the ground, rumpled
And disconnected, marking no particular place,
    Trash to be wadded and stuffed
        Out of sight later, and the dash man
Has slowed to a loose-limbed dance,
    To a shaky aimlessness, his face
        No longer strained into ripples
Like the leading edge of a wing in a wind
    Of his own creation. To have it all
        Be over so suddenly, so abruptly,

So completely, when he had so much more
      In him to offer—he has hardly
            Anything to remember. His body is still wanting
To go on, his mind still racing. What can he be
      Now between the time
            He discovers he's first or second
Or third or out of the running
      And the next time he decides whether he'll fall
            To his knees again on cinders
And try once more or whether he'll take a seat
      With the rest somewhere alone and watch others
            Dashing from start to finish?

The Actress and the Rat

For the last three days I have been ill, now I am kept indoors.
There are insufferable crowds of visitors. Their idle provincial
tongues wag, and I am bored. I rage and rage and envy the rat
that lives under the floor of your theatre.
—written to the actress Olga Leonardovna Knipper, from *The
Letters of Anton Pavlovitch Tchekov* (trans. Constance Garnett)

I can hear her feet overhead. As ever, at night
    She's being somebody else, her voice in a swarm
        Of pleasantries and commands. She's pouting or preening
Or swanning off downstage and gliding back
    To preside over furniture. She's opening
        A purse or a door or her startling eyes and not once
Invading her own privacy. She picks up props
    And graces them with the subtleties of life,
        And in the wings of her theatrical mind
She's measuring those creatures seated beyond
    The lost fourth wall who are watching and listening
        To her being petulant or frightening
Or common or irresistible or more savage
    Than all my dreams of her. I know her words
        Almost as well as she does, having written
Most of them down when she first thought of them
    And having imagined the rest. I wasn't born
        To languish in exile, to devote what little remains
Of my desire to trimming a beard, to rehearsing
    Composure among these overly familiar
        Strangers. Instead, I've been transformed and chosen
Darkness, a hairless tail, a narrow passage,
    And ratness in a maze under her world.
        Now, as the curtains close, I scuttle
To the underside of the floor of her dressing room
    And watch from a neglected corner
        As she rubs away the face of her wicked sister

Or her loving mother or terrible stepmother
Or smug undutiful daughter and becomes
Her irreplaceable self and walks away
Among flowers and laughter. She scatters for me
Half-eaten fruit and sweetmeats. She leaves the promise
Of still another evening under heaven.

Backstage

You're standing behind the scenes in the near darkness
    By a real door set in a canvas wall.
        No one has seen you yet, so you don't exist.
You're waiting for your cue. You can hear the words
    The cast is speaking in what they've agreed to call
        The shape of life this evening, but so far,
You've added nothing but your anxiety.
    You're wearing what you've been told to wear.
        When your time comes, you know exactly how
You're supposed to act, where you're supposed to go
    And how to reveal your character.
        But here, backstage, you mustn't think too much
About anything. Instead, you listen
    To the nearby voices reaching the crucial pause
        When the door beside you opens,
As it does now, and the lights glare
    Down on you and from every side
        Like the eyes you mustn't catch, measuring you
And deciding what you are. You must meet only
    The eyes in the painted faces
        Of people you think you know
By heart, who are saying almost exactly
    What they said last night and will say again tomorrow
        If you're still going to be
This person you've memorized with another name
    Who keeps on being amused by the same events,
        Who never learns how not to be awkward
In the proposal scene, who keeps saying
    The same inadequate lines about love and children
        And death, till you begin
To have a glimmer of what it means
    And what it costs to sit on the dark side
        In those rigid rows and play no part in the story.

At the Door

All actors look for them—the defining moments
When what a character does is what he is.
The script may say, *He goes to the door*
And exits or *She goes out the door stage left.*

But you see your fingers touching the doorknob,
Closing around it, turning it
As if by themselves. The latch slides
Out of the strike-plate, the door swings on its hinges,
And you're about to take that step
Over the threshold into a different light.

For the audience, you may simply be
Disappearing from the scene, yet in those few seconds
You can reach for the knob as the last object on earth
You wanted to touch. Or you can take it
Warmly like the hand your father offered
Once in forgiveness and afterward
Kept to himself.

Or you can stand there briefly, as bewildered
As by the door of a walk-in time-lock safe,
Stand there and stare
At the whole concept of shutness, like a rat
Whose maze has been rebaffled overnight,
Stand still and quiver, unable to turn
Around or go left or right.

Or you can grasp it with a sly, soundless discretion,
Open it inch by inch, testing each fraction
Of torque on the spindles, on tiptoe
Slip yourself through the upright slot
And press the lock-stile silently
Back into its frame.

Or you can use your shoulder
Or the hard heel of your shoe
And a leg-thrust to break it open.

Or you can approach the door as if accustomed
To having all barriers open by themselves.
You can wrench aside
This unauthorized interruption of your progress
And then leave it ajar
For others to do with as they may see fit.

Or you can stand at ease
And give the impression you can see through
This door or any door and have no need
To take your physical self to the other side.

Or you can turn the knob as if at last
Nothing could please you more, your body language
Filled with expectations of joy at where you're going,
Holding yourself momentarily in the posture
Of an awestruck pilgrim at the gate—though you know
You'll only be stepping out against the scrim
Or a wobbly flat daubed with a landscape,
A scribble of leaves, a hint of flowers,
The bare suggestion of a garden.

Curtain Call

After the final scene, the final curtain
    Takes it all back, and here come all the actors
        One more time: the supers and subminors,
Supports and seconds and stars get off their deathbeds
    And stools and telephones and the wobbly cots
        In dressing rooms and out of the smoky alley
(Where they've been understudying
    The moon and the moths) and out of the bathrooms
        (Where they once more missed their dinners),
And they're all meeting upstage out of character
    And coming down together onto the apron
        Under full lights, their bodies their own again,
Silent, joining hands to bow to you
    Once or perhaps more. They're looking left
        And right, down front, toward boxes, up
And out and around, all smiling, all paying attention
    To your palms coming together, to the rattle
        And rustle of programs, coats, and purses, the shuffle
Of feet trying to locate higher centers
    Of balance as seat hinges turn on their own
        And the warm cushions rise to the occasion
From under critical mass. They're listening
    (Harder than you did) to the measures
        Of your approval or indifference, and no matter
What it amounts to, as you sidle off
    And show your backs to them, you'll see their faces
        Already taking care to do without you,
To put a more private distance
    Between you and their words, turning real masks
        Away from you before you can turn yours,
And going beyond sight lines through passages
    Reserved for them alone, before you can reach
        In your preoccupied way the nearest exit.

Quick Meditation on a Senior Citizens' Drill Team

They're putting their whole souls into it left and right
Down hard on the concrete now right now in boots
At roughly the same moment as uniformly
As others in line under orders to feel the beat
Of the drum meaning steady and stomp and remember someone's
Ahead of you and beside you and behind you
Learning to keep their places and their distance
And their balance as an official part of the program
Progressing through familiar tunes to the rattle
Of snares and the clash of cymbals past young people
Who are glad to see you with muffled and mumbled words
Making perfect sense on a line of march determined
Around a corner ahead of time out of sight.

Freak

Her shoulders were so close
Together there was no room
For a ribcage under them
And nowhere in that cage
For two lungs and a heart.
Her hair the color of burlap
Lay soft and thin on a skull
The size of a softball,
And the barker fondled it
With the hollow of his palm
To show how smooth it was
And how round, how small,
How little she had to be
Afraid with as he held her
Firm by the near arm
And gently around her spine
By the other arm. He kept her
Facing our eyes to be sure
We'd see her lips move under
Her ordinary nose
And above her human chin.
Her neck dwindled too soon
To a slip of a girl older
And shorter than we were,
And her eyes stayed shut
As she began her speech,
Which was to say and say
Endlessly an empty
Creekbed of syllables
And to nod as if she meant
To be good. She went on
And on while he explained

She wasn't the only one,
We would find even stranger
Examples of what was missing
From our lives on the other side
Of the sideshow, just imagine
All we had to learn
And we only had to pay
One half of what most people
Would pay for the only show
Beginning before midnight.

The Brief Appearance of the Equable Man

Bells ring as he pays money, and bells ring
As he walks out of the door through extruded music,
And mindful of horns and sirens, he accepts
The key to salvation from a perfect stranger,
Absorbs the slurs of a red-faced man and grows
Old with a gray woman, obeys the law
For a policeman's benefit, blinks at a blind man,
Waits when signaled to wait, then walks, and breathes
Only his fair share of the exhaustion
And refreshment of the city, conferring life
On mannequins under glass and under more glass
Taking a luncheon menu at face value,
Not pausing to reflect on the final offers
In windows where he shares the sky with clouds,
But revolving with a door into a lobby
To drink from a stainless spring, to leave the ground
On a stairway rising under its own power
Like him to greater heights, to a topless tower
Where he allows himself to be led away
And seated at a table not of his choice,
There to be wined and dined, refraining from smoking.

On Seeing a Street Indian Wearing
My Old Dress Suit

It's the one I gave last year to the rummage sale
At the shelter where they get something to eat
Without having to sing. The lapels are sprung,
The pants are up to high water, the fly
Is taking a breather, the side pockets are loaded
Like saddlebags, and instead of a shirt
He's wearing the vest tonight, buttoned one hole
On the bulging bias. The necktie isn't mine
Though I've given away worse.

He's panhandling tourists, walking spraddle-legged
Slightly tilted backward across the path
Of a couple who stop to listen. Their politeness
Surprises him almost sober, turns him almost
Seriously good-humored. He holds out
His palm. He needs a dollar to call his mother.
They fumble to give him coins and then more coins
And sidle around him to go scuttling away.

I wore that suit to plays and operas
And poetry readings and banquets, almost forgetting
How much I had in common with street Indians.
It made me feel safe and sane, not crazy
And dangerous among strangers. It kept me cool.
He's put it on to keep warm, maybe to make
The skin of an enemy useful. And now he sees me
Looking at him and brings the cracked arroyos
Of his palm and face my way. I wonder
What I can possibly find in my new pockets
Besides my hands and some money to buy him off.

In the Kiva at Old Oraibi

This room you stand in has a floor and a ceiling
    And four walls, but its only door is a hatchway
        Overhead where the crooked but smooth
Wind-bleached, deadly-dry gray rungs
    Of a ladder gleam through darkness
        The color of blood. You've let yourself
Down this way, and here you are
    By the cold hearth. At your colder feet
        There are no blue racers, no diamondbacks
Uncoiling like the sun, no sidewinders
    Winding and unwinding among snake priests,
        Sharing their blankets, whispering what the gods
Intend while the days and nights before rain
    Become each other. Now your guide
        Stares down at you from the top of the ladder,
While you stare at nothing, able to offer nothing
    To five of the six directions, one foot braced
        On the lowest rung. He's waiting
For you to take the only way out
    Of the inside of the earth where you don't belong yet.
        A piece of cloudless sky burns blue behind him.

The Houses of the Navajo

They built their hogans out of the way,
Not near a spring, not to frighten
Birds and wild animals, but where
There were no pathways, where a stranger
Would think the land was empty.

The three forked interlocking poles
Slanted toward summer, toward winter,
Toward the death of the sun, but the door
Faced always toward morning.

If someone died in a house, the living
Burned it, burned all of it,
Even the smallest pieces
Where wood was far and hard to find.

They daubed no house with color.
Such houses belonged
Only in legends, only to the gods.

If a rich man's house and a poor man's house
Looked the same, the people said,
These are beautiful
Because they look the same.

In the Room Next Door

The man in the room next door is breaking glass
    Against the wall behind my pillow
        And the shuddering bedstead. He's telling someone
He isn't going to stand for it any more,
    And something or other thumps, goes bump
        In the night on his share of our seventeenth floor
To let us all understand just what he means
    By putting his foot down. And here beginneth
        An extended stretch of stillness interrupted
Only by ugly rumors from the city
    Outside the window, by reconditioned air
        Being grilled and reinvented
Over my head. Suddenly he proclaims
    His perception or comprehension or apprehension
        Of *Bullshit,* hawks and spits, moves furniture
And repeats himself with a raggedly flatulent
    Outburst like a break
        In a water mattress. Now a fresh loud voice
Brings us the news of the healing powers of light,
    Announcing the sale price
        Of plastic blinds going down in many shades
And quickly switches off, while the manager
    Of the night is being sorry to bother them
        But he's had complaints. Would they mind
Keeping it down a little? I lie in wait
    For the end of silence. No doubt, others above me
        And beneath me, who have put themselves out
In cubicles this evening are waiting too,
    Uncertain what will become of us, uncertain
        Where we should go in the morning
If anywhere or whether we should ever
    Put our feet down again. We can hear
        The air arriving, arriving, and water

Running through the walls, unable
   To bring us closer together
      With all the comforts of a home
Away from home, and now a woman is moaning,
   And all of us are listening to a neighbor
      Testing our faith by crying us to sleep.

By the Sea, by the Sea

In the seaside restaurant, they're cracking crabs:
    He's in his thirties, she's eighteen at most.
        She's still in her receptionist's uniform
With a scarf over the name-tag. The candle
    Burning between them is guttering
        Lavender driblets, and both are chewing
Pieces of firm white flesh, while their busy fingers
    Are cracking claws and dipping more in butter.
        She says she's known all along
It would end like this, with him going back to his wife.
    Just like her mother's boyfriend. He says he's sorry
        But she has to understand. She has to be
A matter-of-fact adult, and there's no reason
    They shouldn't enjoy themselves on their last evening.
        They should both be happy they recognized the facts
Of life in time to get up and go on being
    Responsible. She'll see an affair
        Can be just as beautiful as love
If you stop in time, and now she's going to stop
    Crying and take her doggy bag
        And blackberry cobbler and walk on out of here
As if she'd enjoyed herself. They both stand up
    And slowly go down the aisle toward the cashier
        To earn their way outside into the night
Where I follow them (having paid the price
    Of my appetite this evening) and watch them
        To the end of the parking lot and separate cars,
Not kissing good-bye or waving, not even looking.
    Meanwhile, beyond the buttress of driftwood logs
        Where the owners have arranged to keep the sea
And the sand from coming too far ashore, the crabs
    Are facing each other in the rippling shallows
        At low tide, performing mirror dances

On the tips of the inedible parts of their claws,
Some maybe not quite sure
Whether they're mating or fighting
As they face strange partners almost as insane
With longing as they are. They go on dancing
There in the cold salt.

Witness Protection

You've done your duty. You've said for the record
    All you had to say. You've given evidence
        Against the powers, but since they remain
Exactly what they were, you'll have to become
    Two other people. We have a plot for you
        To dwell on, a place for people more or less
Like yourselves, for citizens living in houses
    Next to each other with yards divisible
        By forms of plant life, whose lawns abut
And blend. If you make a similar effort
    To blend in, sooner than you know it,
        You'll find that blending in has changed you
To a second nature. You won't even have to
    Think about it: it won't occur to you
        To do anything much out of the ordinary,
And you'll soon be able to look straight at your neighbors
    From a distance or even right up close
        (At a block party for instance) and you'll say
Exactly what you would have said
    If you were really yourselves, as if you'd rehearsed
        The whole night through. You'll stand there
And say, directly into their open faces,
    Precisely the right words, and they'll look at you
        And smile and believe you and believe in you,
And your characters will be so perfectly
    And permanently established in the design
        Of the neighborhood, you'll forget
To be afraid of being those old selves
    From back in the dangerous time. You'll have children
        Already grown beyond the stage
Of complete dependence, whose value as distractions
    And misdirections will become apparent
        In good time. And if the powers you've betrayed

Come looking for you, they'll only see
Two people so used to being what they are
They couldn't possibly be anything
But this Mother and Father, these two recognizable
And understandable partners
In one small world. Their eyes won't even pause
As they skim across your house, will scarcely glance
Through your picture window. They'll go on searching
For someone else to kill
In the next development, and you'll have done
Your civic duty and made your world a little
Safer and sounder. Once a witness, remember,
Never again a witness. Never again
Will you have to say anything you don't want to say
Except perhaps to yourselves under your breath.

5

The Lost Traveler's Dream: A Sequence

Making Camp

You've found the place in time—no permanent shade,
A level path between your feet and water,
And luck for kindling,
So you drop your pack and begin staying alive
Through the coming night. You haven't indulged yourself
Too long on the trail
To watch the sunlight changing clay and sandstone
To bastions and castle keeps, to vaults of fool's gold,
So you see your way
Clear to the vital stage of rest and shelter.
A man on a journey must be a journeyman.
You make your campfire
First on bare ground (all stones near water are full
To bursting) with a backlog at least as long
As you are tall, a companion
Whose substance will comfort you as it turns to ashes.
Now you may eat whatever seems edible,
And since your weather
For a while to come isn't about to drop
Anything on you from the evening sky,
You may lie down
By the fire and think yourself to sleep
Or think of nothing but sleep or think even harder
Of nothing at all,
Because if you intervene in the open-ended
Discourse between the earth and heaven, the rock
And the hard place, whose discord
Resounds and reverberates in every imaginable
Direction *and* its opposite, the vibrant
Cross talk of earthlings and godlings,
Their babbling and chuckling, moonflies, star-bait, the streakers

Across the belts from Van Allen to Orion,
You'll bring your mysteries
To light again and croak yourself awake
Like the frog in your throat announcing your survival
To the chorus of morning.

Crossing a Path

You see a path in the woods, a well-worn trail
Between and among trees
Where someone has traveled often enough to kill
What lay underfoot,
And all you have to do is follow it
To avoid the dead ends,
The bogging down, the exhaustion, all the self-sour
Nightmares of trail-breaking.
A path says, *Left or right, these are the ways*
Someone wanted to go
Over and over, back and forth from home
To somewhere useful,
Or from somewhere necessary to somewhere safe.
These aren't your ways.
Although you realize the little you find
On your own may be
What no one else has ever wanted to know,
You remember the tree beside you
From its embryo has gone upward and outward
And down and in
And has no need of a pathway since it lives
At its height, at its taproot,
Just under its own circumference, and around
The fire of its heartwood,
And you step across and go on letting each foot
Fall carefully,
Softly and slowly, quietly, yet always
Impulsively, so it leaves
As little trace, as little death as moss
Against moss by nightfall.

At the Edge of a Cliff

You approach it slowly and unwillingly
And so numb in the knees and shuffle-footed,
So tight of breath,
You look behind to be certain no one's pushing
You into this, that it's you alone, so far
At the outer edge,
You might as well be asking to be weighed
In the balance and found wanting, to be headed
Light-headed for judgment,
So you lie down and peek over this cliff,
And something tells you unequivocally,
This is the wrong way.
Once you'd committed yourself to traveling there,
You could change your mind as many times as time
Allowed, but those second thoughts
Would be cut short, discounted at the rate
Of thirty-two feet per second per second while
You were made to feel
What you'd never known in the horizontal world:
The compelling, irrecoverably conclusive
Hands of a living god
Which would pull you and press you home in a fixed position
Like a leaf or a flower or the wings of a butterfly
In a dry arrangement
Suitable for framing, a sentimental comment
On the symmetry of a lifetime, a keepsake
That took your breath away.

Making a Browse Bed

You've reached the end of daylight, and now each step
    You take in the woods is even more unlikely
        To be right than those you spent
Changing your mind and direction
    Under the sun. So having nothing
        Ready-made to sleep on, you make a bed.
The earth and your body both have hidebound views
    On territorial rights: not giving in
        When they meet, either of them,
So you strip the most thickly needled branches
    From the lowest limbs and shingle them, one tier
        After another tier, the length of you,
And caulk them with bushy ends. All of them curved
    Upward once, angling for light,
        So now you turn them down like natural springs.
You've made your bed. Now you must lie in it
    As cautiously as an invalid, interfering
        As little as possible with the shape
Of things to come, and settle down for the night.
    You may add a comfort
        From what you've gathered beside you—the dead leaves
And stems, the spindrift of flowers and ferns,
    The drying cast-offs of the forest floor—
        And spread them over you against the quivering
And the chill, which are sure to come. What happens to you
    Then is, loosely speaking, falling asleep
        As you accept the shelter of your eyelids
And, look, even before you know how to panic
    In those deeper woods on fire behind your forehead,
        You smother the light by closing your mind's eye.

Staying Here

A sliver of light, the crack of morning, breaks
Through your sleep, and your self, returning to its body,
Begins the struggle
Upright to put the night aside, to break camp
Again and walk away, leaving no traces.
But which direction?
Was it between those trees, across that gully,
Or down that stony slope along the river
You'd had firmly in mind
After your heavy thinking by the campfire?
You can't remember, but here, ready and waiting,
As fixed as they ever were,
Are all points of the compass, a spiked wheel
To spur you on your way. You only need
To choose and begin.
Yet something keeps you here. Suddenly Here
Seems irresistibly appealing: Now
And Here, the elixirs
Of life-to-be and life-was, of hope and regret,
Squeezed by time into space, both in your eyes
And hard underfoot—
This clearing, this riverside, this sheltering deadfall,
Last night's charred backlog. Why should you go dragging
Yourself through the woods
Forever in search of something when tomorrow
You could waken and find nothing at all surprising?
The longer you stay
Here, the more completely Here it will be:
Each stone, each bush, each flower, each twist of a branch,
And your own footprints
Will shape a world, and the sounds of wind and water
Will stay the same. You can touch all you remember

And all you hope for.
On the third night or the tenth
Or the thousand-and-first, you will lift your eyes
Out of the haunted blur
Of the firelight toward the darkness and see at last
What has come to find you, kneeling beside you,
Looking at you, waiting for you
To welcome it. Its back will be in shadow
Like yours, its face to the light. You'll know its name
As well as you know your own.

Found

All day, the woods have dwindled. The once almost
    Impenetrable canopy has thinned
        And broken, and now as the light grows,
You suddenly come out into the open,
    Blinking and hesitant,
        And find all of these people running toward you
Clamoring at what you imagine must be
    The sight of a lifetime: your sore eyes
        And even sorer body. They pound your back.
They're rejoicing more than you yourself
    In your mere existence. They seem to believe
        They've rescued you from something.
They all feel wonderful, wonderful. They're all
    Immensely relieved. They can hardly
        Contain themselves. They want to wrap you up
And feed you. They want you to be warm
    And for goodness' sake to calm down.
        They want to feel your pulse
With the ends of their cold fingers. They caress
    Your temples. They pry open
        Your lips and blow their breath into your mouth.
They want to know what you want. They want to know
    How you are. Like overpolite officials
        In a dream of a receiving line, over
And over they ask, *How are you?*
    As if they'd already forgotten
        What you said only a moment ago.
They want to know how it was, how you survived
    The hazardous waste of time, the unknown
        Dangers and glories of being
Lost in the woods, which you remember dimly
    As long ago and far away in another
        Part of a forest

Now lost to you forever. And some are asking
What year it is, as if you alone
Were keeping track. They ask when you were born
As if that's what you'd wanted to find out.
You gaze around at a whole blue sky
Careening with light where birds
Soar overhead and where you can see,
Not just your hand in shadows, but clear miles
Where gods stay at a distance, where nearly nothing
Is in the way of the next step you take
But your desire and the free will
Of your feet. But these people
Clustered near you, offering everything
They can think of, from wildflowers
To love, are holding you.

6

Young Raven

He comes tree-hopping, flapping, half-gliding
    Through hemlock boughs, holding his fat breast
        As lightly as the loose pinfeathers
Trailing him, and clutches a branch
    Hard, balancing, swaying forward
        And back just once and, steady now,
Devotes his full attention to cawing. His voice
    Is high at the upper limits of rawness
        As if blown along the edge
Of a leaf, a whiny fanfare
    Meaning, *This is the place*
        Where I'm still hungry, but the four adults
Who suddenly swoop down and around him—one above,
    Three beyond and below—are keeping their distance,
        Staring at me and indignantly at him
For choosing a perch too near a human being,
    No matter how motionless. They know
        Exactly what I am, but set me aside
To be dealt with later. For now, they sound no alarms,
    But keep their counsel for young raven
        Who squabbles out his orders, his desires,
Announces his new commandments. He opens
    His perfectly smooth black argilite beak,
        As yet unscarred by the resistance
Of the only partially inedible world
    Spread out beneath him, and caws again
        And again. The others stay still,
Crouching at ease, aloof, dead quiet, their eyes
    Gleaming, knowing him. He glances
        Overhead at what must surely be
His mother and left-oblique to his father
    And right-downslope at his attendant cousins,
        Staying once removed, all waiting

For him to do what he was meant to do
     Here and now. He goes on pleading but less
        Urgently, crooking his wings, half-crowing,
Half-yawning, but he finally lets go
     With his lithe dark claws and flutters and flaps
        Down to a smaller tree, staggers headfirst
Among its branches, among its shriveled leaves,
     And poised there now, arranges himself
        Into the shape of Raven Comes to the Feast
And picks and swallows, one after another,
     Overripe black yielding bitter cherries,
        His for the taking.

Robber Jay

You'll never need to search for him
    In the right woods: all you have to do
        Is stand there with your hand out,
And he'll come sailing
    Down from a fir tree silently on an easy
        Glide-path with a flare at the end
As he takes hold of the edge of your cupped palm
    (Your presence beyond that is beside the point)
        With the exact lightness
For his light feet, now both perfectly
    Poised like the rest of him and balanced
        Over your good fortune, old light-boned
Gray-headed Whiskey Jack, the camp-robber,
    Who will take whatever is his
        Or yours without the asking
And spring away on bluntly canopied wings
    Back to his branch which is only
        A springboard to the second
Branch of a journey to a third,
    After which somewhere in the gloom
        Of a crook or hollow
He'll reserve all his impeccable judgment
    On what you've offered and return
        For more, for whatever
You may have left, not just what you may be
    Offering this morning, because he knows you
        Can only have the faintest glimmering
Of the meaning of openhandedness
    And doesn't care whether St. Francis is feeling
        Better about himself and wants to be
Someone else after a friendly handout
    And is doling no more provender, just
        So much and no more. He's coming back

To the party and leaving again
  And coming (bobbing and weaving)
    Back to the party, though it's officially over
And done with, because he's helping it
  And himself go on and on as long
    As it takes to seize the present
And go away and come back for another, for this
  And that and one of those, not biting the hand
    That feeds him or trusting it any longer
Than necessary, except to be there, to keep
  Its place and his, to have and to hold
    Still and be there just once more.

Owl

The crows, a stark black-and-blue whirling
  Murder of them, have treed an owl and are screeching
    At the tops of their sharp voices
And flat from the gut and the ends of their claws
  Against this outrage. They don't want him to be
    There or anywhere. They're proclaiming this evening
Death to all owls, and they're here to tell you
  Owl, owl, owl at the heart of their gyrations,
    Owl in *their* world, and they can hardly
Contain themselves to escalating spirals
  And feints and flaring attacks on the crown of a maple
    Where an owl has made itself
Manifest and motionless: some fly off
  At even louder tangents to other trees
    To scold them in advance for harboring
Future owls. They want to leave no doubt
  In any simple mind: they intend to go on
    Roosting and rousting and treating everything
As murderously as they please, while the owl waits,
  Speckled, shadowed, and still
    As tree bark. The sunlight thins. And now the crows
Are thinning out and heading two by twenty
  And finally three by one toward the rookery
    As the day fades, and the dusk, and the owl
Slowly and silently becomes
  A wide-winged soft-horned shape skimming from under
    The leaning branches and down across the orchard
And over the arch of the arbor by open mouths
  Of morning glories to catch in midair
    The first hummingbird moth of this long night.

Rattlesnake Dance

Though we're both narrow and smooth
        Enough to slip away
Together anywhere
        We could wish when we know love
We rise to sway ourselves
        Erect and begin bulging
Forward bumping our bellies
        Lightly in thrusts and feints
And bows to slow and scaly
        Glissandos passing by
Each other with glancing blows
        And sidelong comings and goings
The tips of our several tongues
        Taking our separate measures
By dividing equally
        Between us the scent of danger
While our hearts are beaten down
        And down into surrender
Undefeated and still
        Devoted to flank attack
We recoil from any further
        Recollection of our mouths
Wide open the fangs unsheathed
        And dripping with sweet venom
Our pale-gray glottal slopes
        Exposed to the light of day
And look how easily
        Our bodies rise once more
To curve and interhinge
        Redoubled as if in anger
Through healing helixes
        Till our open eyes born open

Again can see their ways
   Clear to our charming lives
And we can barely remember
   The rest of ourselves as far
Behind us in this silence
   Grown sharp and brittle now
As flakes of obsidian
   As the chirring of old rattles.

Cow Dance

She would prefer to stand and stare
        Toward the far end of the field
                At the fence where nothing is going to happen
To disturb this good mouthful
        Of grass as she takes time to lower it
                Into her cud. She would far rather
Lie down, but if you insist, she'll move
        Her hoofs and sway the heaviness suspended
                From her level backbone this way
And slowly that. She wouldn't have dreamed
        Of udder-waggling without you or of starting
                A tremor through the blotched job of her hide
Or of trembling her wattle, while at every plump
        Of hoofwork she sounds a thunk-a-clunk
                From a brass bell hanging between her dewlap
And her withers, meaning Old Bossy
        Is on her way again. She wouldn't have risen,
                She wouldn't even have come close
To balancing that mass on her hind legs,
        And don't you suppose she can see almost
                Everyone gaping at her? Why should she
Follow you here or there? Why should she go
        Back there and around here for you? Do you think
                She doesn't know how
Cowlike she seems, how they'll be saying
        She's better at making butterfat
                And cowflops? How they'll say hoofers
Are born, not made, and she doesn't
        Understand the first thing about being
                Light though she goes clumping around
And around as if she might even be
        Happy doing what no one but you
                Wanted her to do? Just look at her

Churning the air and trying her best to smile
    With that mouth which goes too far
        In the wrong directions. Though she may feel
Terrible tomorrow, she'll get over it.
    She got over the moon, didn't she? Well,
        Didn't she? So let's be spoons and dishes.

For a Grizzly Bear Sleeping

He has turned himself and let himself lie down
    And around into this sleep as calmly
        As he would enter a clearing in a forest,
At his ease, as unafraid as ever
    In this safest of all safe places
        Where now no other creature would be so foolish
As to waken him. Through all his dreams he moves
    As freely and as casually as a bear
        Among ripe hazel nuts and berries
And windfall apples, to the strands of honey
    Dangling and dripping down from the torn wax
        Or forward at the quick fishtailing
Of salmon, but always he turns aside
    And lies down in the soft grass of the dream,
        Around the emptiness
Of his full belly where he can lift
    His glistening snout and find, clear on the wind,
        Story after story to tell himself:
Bear enters, becomes contented, and goes away
    Into the next dream. But at the edge of the woods
        He can see in the light ahead
Between the trees something that isn't a tree
    Or a bear moving among them. Now he can smell it,
        And he remembers to turn and run, not afraid
But wise because he has no single place
    Like the bushes crowding against him
        And blundering in his way: without roots
He can take his body to another clearing,
    Even another forest, and though he hears
        The boom louder than the switching and breaking

Of brush under his chest and against his shoulders,
   The surge of his breath, he knows this dream will end
   And he will be lying down in the warm duff
And will curl around himself as perfectly
   Safe and as quiet and as sure
   As he has always been, awake or sleeping.

In the Duck Blind

You don't have to be anything while you're waiting.
    You don't have to look like anything
        But a part of the swamp before dawn
In the duck blind. You don't even have to look out
    Of the slit in this man-made hummock
        Somebody dug in the muck. On its board floor
And under a roof of dead cattails, you can kneel
    Or squat and listen with the ears God gave you
        To tell when a flock of mallards or wigeons
Has come sliding down the air, flaring
    And almost landing, so that you can spring
        Upright and stand and swivel up and around
And fire and fire and reload and fire. You can see them
    Now and can tell by the bursts of feathers
        And suddenly frozen wings, the stilted, half-posed
Silhouettes angling down and slamming
    Against the water. You can almost hear
        The explosions between your cheek and your shoulder,
And you can't imagine anything
    More vital than being
        Again an instrument of the beginning of morning.

The Teal's Wing

Above the tide line, above the dead
    Inchling crabs and the halves of clamshells,
        Beyond the contorted strands of kelp
And seaweed in the sand by a driftwood stump,
    The wing of a teal by itself, severed,
        The iridescence of the wing-patch bright
As the green afterlight of sunset.
    It has been cut neatly. A smooth oval
        Of skin, still pliant, surrounds
The end of the humerus. It can still be
    Stretched (with the help of all your fingers)
        To its short length, to the point
Of its first gray primary feather as if ready
    Now to stroke its missing body forward
        In full flight. The hinge at the ulna
And radius draws the overlapping rows
    Of primaries closed again almost
        Naturally. Even the cartilage
At the fused wristbones and phalanges
    Still moves as if to flare the trailing edge
        For a last landing. If you could see
The rows of barbs on each side of each shaft
    More closely, you might see the barbules
        On each side of them, and the barbicels
On them, perhaps even the hooklets
    On them and looming beyond them
        The ribbons of down—all these almost
Uncountable millions of gestures
    Meant for the wind, for rough and gentle air,
        For the water, for the buoyancy
Of a life still braced and ready,
    Still beautiful, still poised,
        Still light as feathers.

Critical Distance

All game animals know what it is
    Nearly to an inch: how close
        A predator may be allowed to come
Without triggering flight. If they see you
    Far off, they will stand still and wait,
        Staring at you to learn feature by feature
Your shape, your size, your shade,
    The rate at which you may be growing
        Larger than life. Their whole history
Will be trying to puzzle out what you could be
    And what you want, what matters of cold fact
        You're bringing with you, what you've been
Responsible for in the past. They will follow
    Your progress closely. They will consider
        Whether birds in-between
Ignore your slow approach or fly, scolding,
    Around you or try to lead your feet astray
        With their mock injuries. If you maintain
A steady apparently purposeless
    Indirect path and your most indifferent
        Unassuming body language (the playful
Movements you once believed with all your heart
    Would turn you into yourself), you may arrive
        At the invisible defensive line
Only the animals know: exactly how far
    You can be trusted now
        And forever, and they will break and run
And be gone, well out of your reach, out of earshot,
    Out of your sight, and leave you standing
        Your ground, which wasn't your ground

Before, reserving your position and something
  Like your dignity
    For all they're worth and directing
Your attention toward some further points of interest
  Along other lines of approach too numerous
    For you to recall, alone in your own field.

The Principles of Concealment

If you're caught in the open
    In an exposed position, alone,
        Disarmed, and certain you may be
Attacked at any moment, you should settle quickly
    All your differences with whatever lies
        Around you, forcing yourself to agree
With rocks and bushes, trees and wild grass,
    Horses, cows, or sheep, even debris
        To find what you have in common. You no longer
Want to seem what you are, but something
    Harmless and familiar: in a landscape
        Given to greenness and the cold pastels
Of stubble and field stone,
    Protective coloration may be too much
        To hope for, beyond your powers
Like the beatitudes of browsing
    And those conspicuously alarming colors
        That declare you're poisonous
Or taste terrible—all may be doomed
    To fail with an enemy equipped to kill
        From a distance. Your shape betrays you,
And you should try to break it
    With disruptive patterns: if an enemy sees you
        Not as a whole, but as a head distinct
From a torso, as legs or arms
    By themselves, he may ignore you
        And let you have your moment
In the sun as an abstraction gone
    To pieces, as a surface mottled and dappled
        Ambiguously by intercepted light
Like a man canceled. But all these efforts
    Will come to nothing if you move: one gesture
        May catch all eyes. If you stand

Still then, or stay seated
    If you're sitting down, or go on lying
        Down if you're lying, an easy solution
May occur to you, cheek to cheek
    With the hard facts of inorganic life:
        That you have no enemy,
That no one is hunting you,
    That all your precautions were a waste
        Of attention better given to more rewarding
Evasions and pursuits. If so,
    And you take your place again
        As a distinct departure
From your foreground and background,
    You should know it's possible
        For you to feel, after all,
At the first step, at the first crack
    Out of the box, that lethal impact,
        That private personal blow marking your loss
Of the light of day, the companionship
    Of the night, and the creature comforts of home
        As you become a member
Of that other civilization spreading itself
    Around you, ready and able and still
        Called the natural world.

Lying in Ambush

He had been told to wait for the enemy,
    To lie so still, they'd think he was nothing
        But another bush among the weeds and brambles
And fallen leaves. They would come closer
    And closer, their eyes and ears
        Straining to make certain
He didn't exist, and he was to pretend
    He didn't. He was to remain
        Exactly where he was, but not
What he was. Though they might hold him
    Aside like a branch, might even step on him,
        He was to keep his place. And only after
They'd passed him by was he to lift his weapon
    Silently and kill them. But they were so long
        In coming, and he held still so long
With his small pains and itches, with his mismatched
    Arms and legs, with the unlikely angles
        Of his neck and elbows, with the tedium
Of his spinal column, his thirst, with the tempting patterns
    Of daydreams always intermingled
        With the incursions of wrens
And kinglets, he could no longer think
    Of himself at all and woke astonished to find
        The enemy sitting around him, smiling and waiting.

Madstone

When he had killed a white-tailed deer,
A Blackfeet hunter would look first
In its belly, and once in forty winters
One of forty hunters might find
A madstone there the size of a loon's egg,
Dark mother-of-pearl, gleaming.

That hunter would wear it on his breast
At the heart of his breath, and after many days
He would know how to disappear in a thicket
Of sapling birch without touching the ground,
How to stand still
Among the white-flecked gray-black dappling
Of alder bark and not be there,
Would know how to lie down perfectly
Around himself in a hollow of dry grass
And be no more than the light
Of the sun or moon falling through broken stems.

He would know how to stand close to his enemy,
There, meeting those angry eyes
Exactly at that moment, and not feel anger,
Feel nothing, be completely gone
In an instant, out of sight, out of this day's death,
Not through his fear but because he could not remember
How to be foolish.

He would no longer be a hunter but would wander
Carefully in the woods, near the edges of fields
At dawn and dusk, and walk in shallow streams
By half-light. Whatever he ate—
Shoots and berries, the youngest leaves—would turn
And fall within him like his own weather
And gather, layer by thin layer, slowly
In his belly another madstone.

The Murderer

Because he had listened only to his blood,
    Had let it thicken
        Behind his eyes and in his throat
And had killed a man, he could no longer
    Look around at the people. He could speak
        Only in whispers. His hands stayed
Close to his sides and would not reach
    Quickly or far. His food was cold
        At his lips and colder
In his mouth and coldest of all
    When he swallowed and waited
        And waited for anyone who knew his name
To enter the circle of his tipi
    And sit beside him and say, *I remember you.*
        You are sitting by your fire.
I see you. When he would stand
    At last and walk out under the sky at evening
        In his bare feet, the people would see
Only his blanket gathered tight
    At his neck and his empty face
        Above it, no longer shouting or boasting
Or saying what it wanted to say
    But silent. His feet would touch the worn clay
        Or the dirt ahead of him
Slowly as if not willing to be
    Heavy, as if unwilling to move
        The grass aside or bend it too suddenly
Or sharply near the roots, not wanting to end
    The lives of anything, not even Ant
        Or Beetle. He would feel the wind
Against him and around him
    But not through his uncombed hair. He would know
        The ghost of the dead man was nearby

Ready to send that wind from behind the hunters
To the buffalo to warn them and turn them away
Even in the night, and the tethered horses
Would hear him alone at night, far from the campfires,
Singing, and the people would hear him singing
And crying out to himself
And would listen and do nothing,
And when he had been a murderer
Long enough, the one who had most loved
The dead man would come close, would look at him
Closely and touch his shoulder
And say, *You may be yourself now.*
And he would try to remember how
To walk and speak and look around at the people
Again and be himself among them.

Dream House

They would sit together under the low roof
    Crouched close, holding
        Their chests close to their thighs,
Their knees to their chins, having left behind
    The dim daylight to come into this house
        To dream, even those few
Who were almost never silent
    Or those who had only begun to say
        Their first thoughts—all would sit still
And wait. All would listen
    To the nothing of breathing
        Till they no longer knew the names
Of the shapes around them
    Where there was nothing to hear or see
        Except what would come drifting
Across the other eyes
    Behind their eyes. The first fires and voices
        Would sputter and whisper, glisten
And murmur together, shimmer
    And grow faint, then dazzle again
        And suddenly wear bone masks and dance
Or be born and die
    Once more. They would breathe deeply,
        Holding their knees, their arms clasping
Only themselves, and would wait, not singing,
    And from among them someone old
        Or young, a woman or hunter or sickly brother
Or a girl who had become a fish
    Or a bird, would cry out loud
        What was lying beneath the ice
Under them, what was becoming bubbles rising
    Through a coldness like green stone,
        And would say those words, and others

Would say them, and still other voices
        Would say new words. They would hear them
                Pouring together, crying out more words,
And one would sing words melting
        Or words hard, the bubbles breaking
                Out of breath, out of breath,
And the shape of the song
        For the seasons to come would turn clear
                In the darkness where all forty souls
Of Little Diomede Island would know now
        The holy song of the new year
                Which would send the fishermen out onto the ice
And over the deepest water and guide them
        And give them luck and bring them back again
                Alive to the safe shore.

Telling What Happened

The Kwakiutl said one word,
L!aaso, only one
        To mean from that moment
To the end of the next silence:
        I have seen a sacred apparition
                In the woods. It happened to them
So often, they needed no more
        Than that one word to say it
                When they sat by the fire
Or lay down as the fire was dying,
        Whispering it to themselves
                Or to one Other
Lying near. That day
        When one had carried home
                The memory of a fern
Lifting itself again
        Like a green wing through ice,
                Returning through that heaviness
And melting without changing,
        Its feathers the first above the cloud
                Of the frozen snow. Or the memory
Of fog closing the cedar branches
        Overhead into a whiteness
                Like a melting snowdrift rising
And drifting as lightly
        As its own cloud. Or the red eyelets
                Of moss suddenly gleaming
Like firelight in the frost,
        Like the eyes of the ermine turning
                To look without moving
Its lifted forepaw
        Yet disappearing without touching
                The earth or the air. Or the light

Itself in their hands, over their hands,
   Falling as if on leaves
     And burning as darkly
As what opens and remains
   Open behind the closed eyes
     Of the horned owl. They would say
L!aaso, only one word, and the other
   Nearby in the night would know
     It was safe to sleep now.

That Child

That child was dangerous. That just-born
    Newly washed and silent baby
        Wrapped in deerskin and held warm
Against the side of its mother could understand
    The language of birds and animals
        Even when asleep. It knew why Bluejay
Was scolding the bushes, what Hawk was explaining
    To the wind on the cliffside, what Bittern had found out
        While standing alone in marsh grass. It knew
What the screams of Fox and the whistling of Otter
    Were telling the forest. That child knew
        The language of Fire
As it gnawed at sticks like Beaver
    And what water said all day and all night
        At the creek's mouth. As its small fingers
Closed around Stone, it held what Stone was saying.
    It knew what Bear Mother whispered to herself
        Under the snow. It could not tell
Anyone what it knew. It would laugh
    Or cry out or startle or suddenly stare
        At nothing, but had no way
To repeat what it was hearing, what it wanted most
    Not to remember. It had no way to know
        Why it would fall under a spell
And lie still as if not breathing,
    Having grown afraid
        Of what it could understand. That child would learn
To sit and crawl and stand and begin
    Putting one foot forward and following it
        With the other, would learn to put one word

It could barely remember slightly ahead
Of the other and then walk and speak
And finally run and chatter,
And all the Tillamook would know that child
Had forgotten everything and at last could listen
Only to people and was safe now.

The Sick Child

That child was quiet and would no longer run
Or shout or throw stones. It wanted to lie down
In daylight and try to dream,
Closing its eyes, turning away from its food.
It would no longer look
At fire or the sky. It had forgotten how
To listen and drink water. They asked the Dreamer
To walked into the woods and hunt for its soul
Which had wandered away
And not come back. The Dreamer searched
Under the arching fronds of deerfern
And lifted apart the matted tangles
Of bedstraw. He fumbled in the hollows
Of fallen hemlocks where deer mice
And ground squirrels had made nests
To tempt a soul into hiding. He hunted
Under the overhanging banks of springs
Where white crowfoot had toppled forward
Into the clear water and could hardly remember
It belonged to its roots and could only grow
Down a small spillway at the beginning
Of a rivulet toward a creek and a river. But the Dreamer
Returned alone, and that child went on
Burning under its skin, turned cold,
Then shut its mouth forever, its breath broken.
Its mother put salmon and sweet salmon berries
And all its clothing into the fire
And told it to go now with its father,
To go with its name and its body out the doorway
And never to come back again in the night.

Carrying the Fire

He had felt fevered, even in the wind
    Blowing across the sand and the salt marsh,
        Even in the chill of night, not the simmering
Of a full stomach, not the sunlit breath
    From guiding a canoe among waves, but a heaviness
        Like the gathering of a blanket
Of ashes over his shoulders, like the heat
    Of a charred backlog, of firestones, of a sun
        Even before the sun had risen,
And in the morning, the real morning, he knew
    From the eyes of those around him,
        From their sudden distance, even the eyes
Of his wife and children, as he struggled
    To rise by the dead fire and stand still,
        That in his sleep he had been given
The Mask of Many Holes. So he said good-bye
    Without touching, picked up his knife and bowl,
        His fishing spear and barbed fishhooks
Bought from the Iron People, gathered together
    A driftwood raft and a branch, and rowed himself
        Across the narrow inlet to Graveyard Spit
And crawled ashore and, still able to rise,
    Walked among beach grass and the empty halves
        Of clams and scallops to the fallen forest,
All stripped of its bark, all heaped by the tide,
    And sat down in that shelter, facing the water,
        And waited there for days like a nesting bird
Warming its young. And the gulls came
    And waited with him, knowing what he was
        And what he would become, knowing already
His new name before he had dreamed it
    In the night as he watched the Clallam campfires burning,
        As he himself was burning, then going out.

Making a God

His god let people die and had not stayed
    Under his fingers in the night
        Or in the morning, under the sun
In the afternoon or by the fire at evening,
    So he made his god out of clay
        And kept it with him. Though he painted it
The colors of sea and sky
    And dressed it in cowrie shells and feathers
        From the sea and sky, it melted
In the rain and cracked in the sun, and he lost it
    Somewhere among palm trees. So he carved his god
        Again out of hard wood,
A seated god still light enough
    To carry through the long day and by firelight
        And into sleep till sunrise
Without melting. Though he put flowers
    On each side of its head, his god could hear
        Nothing with them and let the people die,
Let his mother and father die and his wife die
    And his children sicken and die,
        So he made another god out of stone
With shut eyes weeping, whose tears
    As they fell were slowly changing
        Into stone people, being born
While falling and laughing and lying
    Around its feet, and his god was lifting them up
        In both of its stone hands and eating them.

The Elders

When by the fire at sundown the elders
    No longer spoke, no longer
        Shook their heads or reached for the food
Put down beside them, when their eyes stayed closed
    Or open without blinking,
        When they no longer saw or heard
What they were asked to understand, their children
    Would cover them and let them lie
        Close to the embers and would turn them over
Carefully and gently in the night
    As they would have turned themselves
        If they had been sleeping
And would let them rest there through the day
    To be covered with leaves in rain,
        To be dried by the sun
Like clothing newly washed in a spring,
    And then would bring them to the fire again
        At evening, to their accustomed places
As the warmth and light of the flames
    Healed them, as the smoke healed them and the ashes
        Smoothed across their faces, across their arms
And legs and over their whole bodies
    Healed them slowly night after night and morning
        And afternoon, till the bundles of their skin
Grew light around their bones, still lighter
    Each time they were lifted
        And carried through the forest to a new campfire,
Till even the youngest could lift them
    Like those just born. Their eyes would be changed
        To cowrie shells, to slits in a whiteness
Able to see more clearly into the sky
    Even at night and far below the earth,
        As far upstream as the source and as far

Downstream as the dark mouth of the Sepik River,
    Till their spirits became large birds flying away,
        Not into trees or into the clouds
But straight against the shoulder blades of their children
    Where they would hold as tight against their spines
        As if they had grown there, down-curved beaks
Firm along the tops of the living skulls
    Of those grown children, where they would wait
        And whisper whatever children need to know.

The People Who Ate Snow

The sun died. The birds and animals died.
Winter was too strong, too hard. The Aleut gave in
And began to eat snow, ate nothing but snow,
A sweetness more certain than the breasts of birds,
And winter began burning. They held their fingers
Around it till it became their firelight.
They sat and feasted all day and all night, lifting
Snow, more snow to their mouths, no longer trembling
But turning their faces and bodies toward that fire.
They dreamed around it, fearless and motionless.

How It Will Be

When we are changed to minnows in a river
    As Smoholla said we would be
        To his Ghost Dancers, we will know
How to hold still, to be only
    Here in the same place
        This instant and this instant,
To be blurred like the water
    With all its changing pathways, its catchings
        Of slope and light, to have our eyes
Open and always open, and at evening
    When we sidle into shallows
        Almost as slow as pools
And what divides us from the other world
    Gleaming above the surface
        Settles into a sky where the sun
Grows longer and disappears
    And the long moon
        Turns round and the creatures living
Above the sky come down
    To touch the skin of heaven,
        We can learn to touch it too.
We will know what we have never known,
    Will know it so clearly,
        We will know enough to remain
Small and hungry, to see
    The long sun come again and learn
        The sharp beak of Heron
And the quick huge shadow of Loon
    And the scuttling of Otter,
        Yet go on being ourselves. The current
Will darken and brighten, turn warm and cold,
    Be suddenly filled with the strange dead
        Or the even stranger living, will slow

Or quicken, burn or sweeten, turn salt
    Or harden till all but its deepest bed stops moving
        Or rises till it blunders over a wilderness
Of flowers and weeds, so broad it doesn't remember
        How to be a river and then shrinks
            Almost to nothing, so narrow
We must become more than what is left of our bodies
    And will see and become what is always
        Rushing toward us and around us.

Acknowledgments

The poems in this book appeared originally in the following periodicals and are reprinted with their permission:

American Poetry Review: "The Path," "Thoreau and the Toads," "Thoreau and the Body," "Thoreau and the Catfish," "Thoreau and the Cow," "The First Passenger Balloon Ascension, 1783," "How It Will Be," "Dream House," "Dr. Frankenstein's Garden," "In the Experimental Pool," "Witness Protection," and "Night Light"

Amicus Journal: "Making Camp"

Atlantic Mc 'hly: "Lachrymals"

Black Warrior Review: "Keeping Quiet at the Benedictine Abbey"

Chariton Review: "The Houses of the Navajo," "A Homily for the Preservation of the Spirit in a Time of Dread," "The Joggers," and "The People Who Ate Snow"

Dark Horse Review: "Slug," "Speeding," and "The Murderer"

Denver Quarterly: "Quick Meditation on a Senior Citizens' Drill Team" and "Curtain Call"

The English Journal: "The Weather Man," "Dancing Daughters," and "Moth Flight"

Free Lunch: "Making a Browse Bed"

The Georgia Review: "Staying Here," "At the Edge of a Cliff," "Critical Distance," and "The End of the Story"

The Gettysburg Review: "Elegy on the First Day of Spring"

Hampden-Sydney Review: "The Book of Moonlight" and "In the Duck Blind"

Hanging Loose: "Forgetting the Magic Words" and "In the Kiva at Old Oraibi"

The Hudson Review: "My Father and the Hydrostatic Paradox" and "The Collectors"

Iowa Review: "In a Country Cemetery"

The Kenyon Review: "The Teal's Wing," "Telling What Happened," and "Robber Jay"

The Nation: "For a Mockingbird"

New Letters: "Cow Dance" and "By the Sea, by the Sea"

The New Republic: "The Brief Appearance of the Equable Man"

Ohio Review: "Symposium," "Found," "In the Snow," and "On Seeing a Street Indian Wearing My Old Dress Suit"

Ontario Review: "Alexandra and the Thunder," "Rattlesnake Dance," and "Aerial Act"

Paris Review: "The Lessons of Water," "God and Man and Flower," "Thoreau Wading in a River," and "Howl"

Partisan Review: "Making a God"

Ploughshares: "Thoreau and the Crickets"

Poetry: "Landscaping Rocks for Sale," "Crossing a Path," "The Principles of Concealment," "Madstone," "The House of Song," "Thinking of What to Say," "The Words-and-Music Men," "The Elders," "A Girl Playing in a Sandbox," "That Child," "Lying in Ambush," "The Sick Child," "Carrying the Fire," "The Son of a Glover," "For Laurel and Hardy on My Workroom Wall," and "Wallace Stevens on His Way to Work"

Prairie Schooner: "At the Ruins of Baalbek, 1971," "Waiting Out a Storm on a Deserted Farm," "Benjamin Franklin and the Dust Devil," and "Looking into a Crystal Ball"

River City Review: "On Thin Ice"

Sewanee Theological Review: "Meeting the Ditchdigger," "Meditation," and "In the Room Next Door"

Shenandoah: "Young Raven," "In the Shade of the Old Apple Tree," "For a Grizzly Bear Sleeping," "Wild Cucumber," and "The Actress and the Rat"

A Smartish Pace: "Our Hands" and "The Loneliness of the 100-Meter Dash Man"

The Southern Review: "The Four Fates"

Threepenny Review: "The Landscaper" and "Freak"

Triquarterly: "At the Door," "High Steel," and "Owl"

Verse: "Dead Letter from Out of Town"

The Yale Review: "Thoreau and the Stumps" and "Backstage"

Illinois Poetry Series
Laurence Lieberman, Editor

History Is Your Own Heartbeat
Michael S. Harper (1971)

The Foreclosure
Richard Emil Braun (1972)

The Scrawny Sonnets and Other
Narratives
Robert Bagg (1973)

The Creation Frame
Phyllis Thompson (1973)

To All Appearances: Poems New and
Selected
Josephine Miles (1974)

The Black Hawk Songs
Michael Borich (1975)

Nightmare Begins Responsibility
Michael S. Harper (1975)

The Wichita Poems
Michael Van Walleghen (1975)

Images of Kin: New and Selected
Poems
Michael S. Harper (1977)

Poems of the Two Worlds
Frederick Morgan (1977)

Cumberland Station
Dave Smith (1977)

Tracking
Virginia R. Terris (1977)

Riversongs
Michael Anania (1978)

On Earth as It Is
Dan Masterson (1978)

Coming to Terms
Josephine Miles (1979)

Death Mother and Other Poems
Frederick Morgan (1979)

Goshawk, Antelope
Dave Smith (1979)

Local Men
James Whitehead (1979)

Searching the Drowned Man
Sydney Lea (1980)

With Akhmatova at the Black Gates
Stephen Berg (1981)

Dream Flights
Dave Smith (1981)

More Trouble with the Obvious
Michael Van Walleghen (1981)

The American Book of the Dead
Jim Barnes (1982)

The Floating Candles
Sydney Lea (1982)

Northbook
Frederick Morgan (1982)

Collected Poems, 1930–83
Josephine Miles (1983; reissue, 1999)

The River Painter
Emily Grosholz (1984)

Healing Song for the Inner Ear
Michael S. Harper (1984)

The Passion of the Right-Angled Man
T. R. Hummer (1984)

Dear John, Dear Coltrane
Michael S. Harper (1985)

Poems from the Sangamon
John Knoepfle (1985)

In It
Stephen Berg (1986)

The Ghosts of Who We Were
Phyllis Thompson (1986)

Moon in a Mason Jar
Robert Wrigley (1986)

Lower-Class Heresy
T. R. Hummer (1987)

Poems: New and Selected
Frederick Morgan (1987)

Furnace Harbor: A Rhapsody of the
North Country
Philip D. Church (1988)

Bad Girl, with Hawk
Nance Van Winckel (1988)

Blue Tango
Michael Van Walleghen (1989)

Eden
Dennis Schmitz (1989)

Waiting for Poppa at the Smithtown
Diner
Peter Serchuk (1990)

Great Blue
Brendan Galvin (1990)

What My Father Believed
Robert Wrigley (1991)

Something Grazes Our Hair
S. J. Marks (1991)

Walking the Blind Dog
G. E. Murray (1992)

The Sawdust War
Jim Barnes (1992)

The God of Indeterminacy
Sandra McPherson (1993)

Off-Season at the Edge of the World
Debora Greger (1994)

Counting the Black Angels
Len Roberts (1994)

Oblivion
Stephen Berg (1995)

To Us, All Flowers Are Roses
Lorna Goodison (1995)

Honorable Amendments
Michael S. Harper (1995)

Points of Departure
Miller Williams (1995)

Dance Script with Electric Ballerina
Alice Fulton (reissue, 1996)

To the Bone: New and Selected
Poems
Sydney Lea (1996)

Floating on Solitude
Dave Smith (3-volume reissue, 1996)

Bruised Paradise
Kevin Stein (1996)

Walt Whitman Bathing
David Wagoner (1996)

Rough Cut
Thomas Swiss (1997)

Paris
Jim Barnes (1997)

The Ways We Touch
Miller Williams (1997)

The Rooster Mask
Henry Hart (1998)

The Trouble-Making Finch
Len Roberts (1998)

Grazing
Ira Sadoff (1998)

Turn Thanks
Lorna Goodison (1999)

Traveling Light:
Collected and New Poems
David Wagoner (1999)

Some Jazz a While:
Collected Poems
Miller Williams (1999)

The Iron City
John Bensko (2000)

Songlines in Michaeltree: New and
Collected Poems
Michael S. Harper (2000)

Pursuit of a Wound
Sydney Lea (2000)

The Pebble: Old and New Poems
Mairi MacInnes (2000)

Chance Ransom
Kevin Stein (2000)

House of Poured-Out Waters
Jane Mead (2001)

The Silent Singer: New and Selected
Poems
Len Roberts (2001)

The Salt Hour
J. P. White (2001)

Guide to the Blue Tongue
Virgil Suárez (2002)

The House of Song
David Wagoner (2002)

National Poetry Series

Eroding Witness
Nathaniel Mackey (1985)
Selected by Michael S. Harper

Palladium
Alice Fulton (1986)
Selected by Mark Strand

Cities in Motion
Sylvia Moss (1987)
Selected by Derek Walcott

The Hand of God and a Few
Bright Flowers
William Olsen (1988)
Selected by David Wagoner

The Great Bird of Love
Paul Zimmer (1989)
Selected by William Stafford

Stubborn
Roland Flint (1990)
Selected by Dave Smith

The Surface
Laura Mullen (1991)
Selected by C. K. Williams

The Dig
Lynn Emanuel (1992)
Selected by Gerald Stern

My Alexandria
Mark Doty (1993)
Selected by Philip Levine

The High Road to Taos
Martin Edmunds (1994)
Selected by Donald Hall

Theater of Animals
Samn Stockwell (1995)
Selected by Louise Glück

The Broken World
Marcus Cafagña (1996)
Selected by Yusef Komunyakaa

Nine Skies
A. V. Christie (1997)
Selected by Sandra McPherson

Lost Wax
Heather Ramsdell (1998)
Selected by James Tate

So Often the Pitcher Goes to Water
until It Breaks
Rigoberto González (1999)
Selected by Ai

Renunciation
Corey Marks (2000)
Selected by Philip Levine

Manderley
Rebecca Wolff (2001)
Selected by Robert Pinsky

Other Poetry Volumes

Local Men and *Domains*
James Whitehead (1987)

Her Soul beneath the Bone: Women's
Poetry on Breast Cancer
Edited by Leatrice Lifshitz (1988)

Days from a Dream Almanac
Dennis Tedlock (1990)

Working Classics: Poems on
Industrial Life
*Edited by Peter Oresick and
Nicholas Coles* (1990)

Hummers, Knucklers, and Slow
Curves: Contemporary Baseball
Poems
Edited by Don Johnson (1991)

The Double Reckoning of Christopher
Columbus
Barbara Helfgott Hyett (1992)

Selected Poems
Jean Garrigue (1992)

New and Selected Poems, 1962–92
Laurence Lieberman (1993)

The Dig and *Hotel Fiesta*
Lynn Emanuel (1994)

For a Living: The Poetry of Work
*Edited by Nicholas Coles and
Peter Oresick* (1995)

The Tracks We Leave: Poems on
Endangered Wildlife of North America
Barbara Helfgott Hyett (1996)

Peasants Wake for Fellini's *Casanova*
and Other Poems
*Andrea Zanzotto; edited and translated
by John P. Welle and Ruth Feldman;
drawings by Federico Fellini and
Augusto Murer* (1997)

Moon in a Mason Jar and *What My Father Believed*
Robert Wrigley (1997)

The Wild Card: Selected Poems, Early and Late
Karl Shapiro; edited by Stanley Kunitz and David Ignatow (1998)

Turtle, Swan and *Bethlehem in Broad Daylight*
Mark Doty (2000)

Illinois Voices: An Anthology of Twentieth-Century Poetry
Edited by Kevin Stein and G. E. Murray (2001)

On a Wing of the Sun
Jim Barnes (3-volume reissue, 2001)

The University of Illinois Press
is a founding member of the
Association of American University Presses.

Composed in 9/13 Cheltenham
with Nofret display
by Celia Shapland
for the University of Illinois Press
Designed by Paula Newcomb
Manufactured by Thomson-Shore, Inc.

University of Illinois Press
1325 South Oak Street
Champaign, IL 61820-6903
www.press.uillinois.edu